ESSENTIALS OF MANAGEMENT

PRACTICAL BANK MANAGEMENT

ESSENTIALS OF MANAGEMENT

PRACTICAL BANK MANAGEMENT

Kenneth Toft

B.Com. M.Sc. (Econ.), A.I.B., M.B.I.M.

Head of the Department of Economics and Banking

City of London Polytechnic

MACDONALD AND EVANS

MACDONALD & EVANS LTD.
Estover, Plymouth PL6 7PZ

First published 1977

ISBN: 0 7121 1664 8

Printed in Great Britain by
Clarke Doble and Brendon Ltd. Plymouth

General Editor's Foreword

Books in the Essentials of Management series are designed for the executive director, manager, accountant, company secretary, administrator; in fact, anyone who is concerned with improving business efficiency.

Inevitably these "professionals" are busy men or women with limited free time at their disposal. Yet they must understand the latest techniques, principles, practices and developments thus enabling them to apply appropriate skills to the problems which arise.

In designing the books in this series we have concentrated on presenting the facts in an interesting and stimulating way, combining principles and practice. Case studies are integrated into the text, showing the real problems which may arise in the world of industry or commerce.

General Editor

Preface

This is a small book – small in size as well as pretensions. The management expert will find it unsatisfying, the marketing man light weight. The corporate planner will scoff, the backroom boffin – constructing a mathematical model and toying with computer programmes – will mock.

But this is not written for them, the experts.

These words are for the general banker, in particular for the young banker: the objective to show that banking is more than a routine occupation requiring advanced technical expertise.

Banking is big business and as such it success demands the application of advanced management skills and techniques. Routine is important, technical knowledge is vital, but management art and science provides a new dimension, one which gives banking a creativity not always apparent to those immersed in its daily problems.

A small book maybe, but hopefully a controversial and stimulating book which will play a part in improving the business of banking and the careers of those engaged in it.

1977 K.T.

Acknowledgments

Whilst accepting full responsibility for the contents of this work, it would be churlish not to acknowledge the debt I owe to all those who, directly and indirectly, contributed to its writing.

Firstly, to the many men and women whose managerial skills I have observed during my working life in banking and education.

Secondly, to J. W. Gilbart (1794–1863), the first General Manager of the London and Westminster Bank, whose views on bank administration may still be read with profit and some of whose words of wisdom appear at the head of the following chapters.

Finally, to the many writers on banking and management subjects whose works are found in the libraries of the Institute of Bankers and the City of London Polytechnic.

Contents

General Editor's Foreword v
Preface vii
Acknowledgments ix
List of Illustrations xiii
Introduction: How are you managing? xv

I. Corporate Planning 1
- What is a system?
- Should a system have objectives?
- Banking as a system
- Bank services
- Bank objectives
- Bank profits
- Input and output in profitable balance
- The black box
- What does top management do?
- Does size affect management?
- How to make a profit?
- Management style
- Management in a changing world

II. Planning and Control 13
- Functions of management
- Leadership
- Planning
- The corporate plan
- Formal or informal plan?
- Long-term objectives
- Medium-term needs
- Costing
- Control
- Look at the time scale
- Monitoring progress

III Line Management 24
- Breaking down the corporate plan
- The operational plan
- Branch management
- The management approach

IV. Communicating Information 32
Harmony of objectives
A system's needs
Internal information
Return on capital
Budgetary control
Why communicate?
Charts and diagrams
Effective communication

V. Managing Human Resources 49
Human resources
Motivation
Human relations
Management by objectives
Human development
Job enrichment
Job analysis
Job descriptions

VI. Bank Marketing 61
The marketing approach
Production orientation
Marketing mix
Seeking attitudes
Product marketing
Branch marketing
Public relations

VII. The Tools of Management 72
Developing a management attitude
Organisation
Management techniques
Planning charts
Critical path analysis
Decision-taking
Using these tools to good effect

Index 87

List of Illustrations

1. A hierarchy of systems 3
2. A bank's output 4
3. A bank's profit 6
4. A bank's input 15
5. A bank system 16
6. Planning Information 34
7. Communicating progress 40
8. Communicating information 42
9. A communication system 45
10. Outline job description 58
11. Profit planning 62
12. Product life cycle for a bank service 64
13. Organisation charts: role of the deputy manager 74
14. Flow chart: bank lending 76
15. Critical path analysis: a credit card launch 80

Introduction

HOW ARE YOU MANAGING?

That's the sort of question a lot of people could be asked: a newly-married daughter by her mother, a bank manager by his regional controller, a newly-appointed general manager by the bank chairman.

In a sense, we are all managers: we have our life to live and have to decide what to do with it. Sometimes we drift, giving little thought to the future; sometimes we take decisions that will have far-reaching consequences for our future happiness and prosperity.

Throughout our lives we have to take decisions: we have to decide how to spend our time each day, how to spend our limited income. Our freedom of choice is also limited: time has to be spent sleeping and most of us have to work. A large part of our income goes on food, clothes and housing. Often our decisions are made on the spur of the moment; often our decision is to do nothing and to let events take their course. But however we play it, ultimately we are responsible for managing our own affairs.

A clear and simple parallel can be drawn – take the housewife as an example. Her limited resources have to be allocated to the best advantage, the day-to-day running of the home has to be planned and controlled, a suitable environment and atmosphere has to be created in which the family can live and develop. She also needs technical knowledge: how to provide a balanced diet, keep clothes clean, do the shopping.

In a similar way, every manager has to combine management ability with technical skill, and the more senior he becomes the more important are these aspects of his job.

Compare the problems faced by the branch managers of a bank, a supermarket and an insurance company. The management skills required in each case are broadly the same: staff have to be organised so that the branch runs effectively and efficiently, and in each case the manager is responsible to someone higher up the hierarchy for the work he does. But the technical knowledge and skill required in each case is quite different. The bank manager needs to know how to grant an overdraft and take security, the supermarket manager how to ensure that he has an adequate supply of the right goods properly displayed and the insurance manager how to underwrite a risk and quote the correct premium.

In this book you will read little about technical skills. If you want to know about lending money, undertaking foreign business or operating a customer's account, you must go elsewhere. We are concerned with the art and skills of management and how these can be applied in the banking context. You should find nothing difficult to understand, but when you have finished you should be further on the way to becoming a good manager.

CHAPTER I

Corporate Planning

"The basic principles for the conduct of banking have not changed radically since Gilbart's day. He, too, saw that profit was related to the efficient use of resources: many of his rules for efficient management practice find a place in modern text books, although expressed in rather different language."

John Prideaux, Chairman, National Westminster Bank, 1972

WHAT IS A SYSTEM?

A bank is a *system* established for a particular reason. There are many types of system and they serve many purposes: a power station is a system for producing electricity, a retail shop is a system for providing a service.

One vitally important feature of systems is that they have *inputs* and *outputs*: the body's digestive system for example, receives inputs of food and, by mechanical and chemical processes, yields outputs of vitamins, carbohydrates and other materials vital for the body's nutrition. The input of one system frequently derives from the output of others and its own output then becomes the input of yet another system in the chain. In this case the total integrated set of systems forms the human body and this itself may be regarded as a system enabling life to continue.

SHOULD A SYSTEM HAVE OBJECTIVES?

Men have constructed systems to serve many purposes, the type of system being determined by the end in view. If the aim is to produce cars, a factory will be planned and built and machinery installed. Raw materials, labour and components will be fed into the system, operations will commence and there will be an output of cars. However, in a wider sense, a car production plant may be regarded only as a sub-system, that is as part of a total manufacturing system which itself forms part of the country's whole economic system.

Probably it is changes in the economic system that have led to the plant being constructed in the first place, an increase in demand for cars signalling that profits can be increased if production is stepped up. For successful system design there must be a clear definition of the objectives to be achieved.

BANKING AS A SYSTEM

A country's economy is as we have already seen composed of many dependent systems and sub-systems. Among them is the banking system. Banking activity is itself a chain of dependent parts – there is the central banking system, the commercial banking system and the merchant banking system. One particular bank is a sub-system of the whole. It forms part of a higher-level structure and is itself made up of a large series of other systems. Figure 1 shows how a bank is placed within this hierarchy.

The name we give to a system is determined by its output. If a system is producing cars or aircraft we would not call it a bank. Indeed it is difficult to think of circumstances where a system producing goods would be referred to as a bank, the role of a bank being to provide a service. But there are many types of service, and banks normally concern themselves only with financial services: services like cleaning clothes and extracting teeth they leave to others!

BANK SERVICES

The precise nature of the banks' financial services differs between institutions and between groups of institutions. And the services change over time. In recent years there

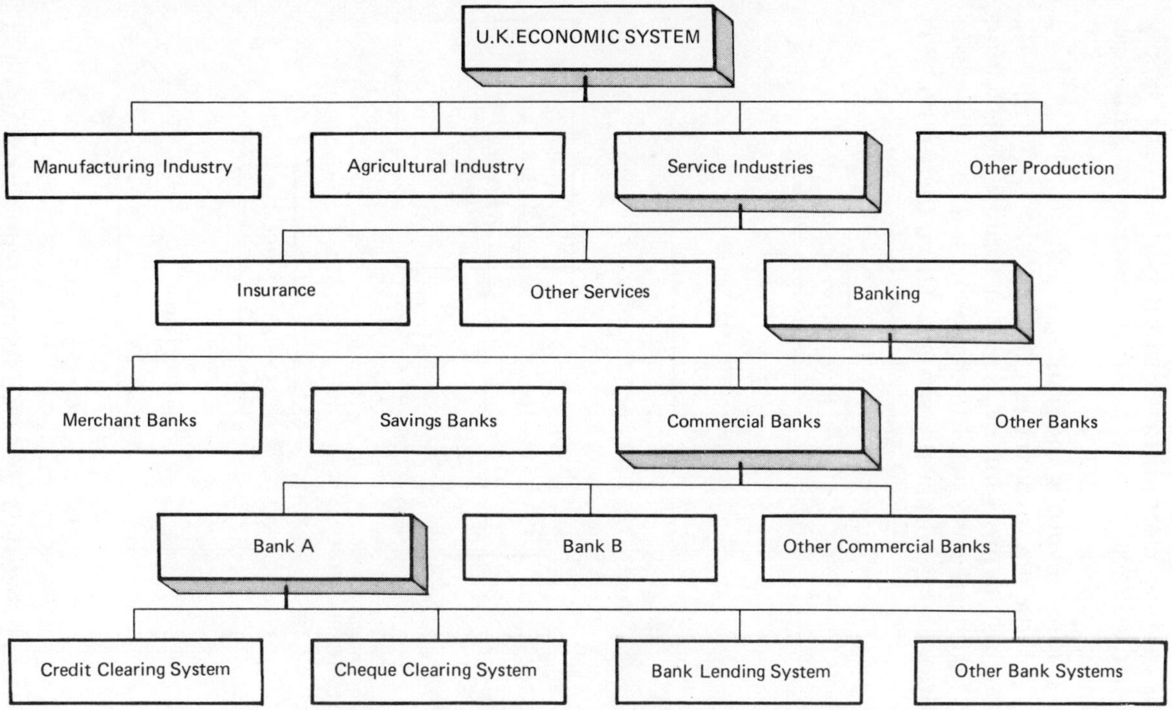

Fig. 1. A hierarchy of systems.

has been a great increase in the variety of bank services and it has become more difficult to categorise a bank simply by what it provides. It is possible, however, to distinguish two main types:

1. those involving the grant of credit;
2. those not involving it.

Clearly, the provision of overdraft facilities falls within the first category, whilst the provision of night-safe facilities comes within the second. Often there is no clear

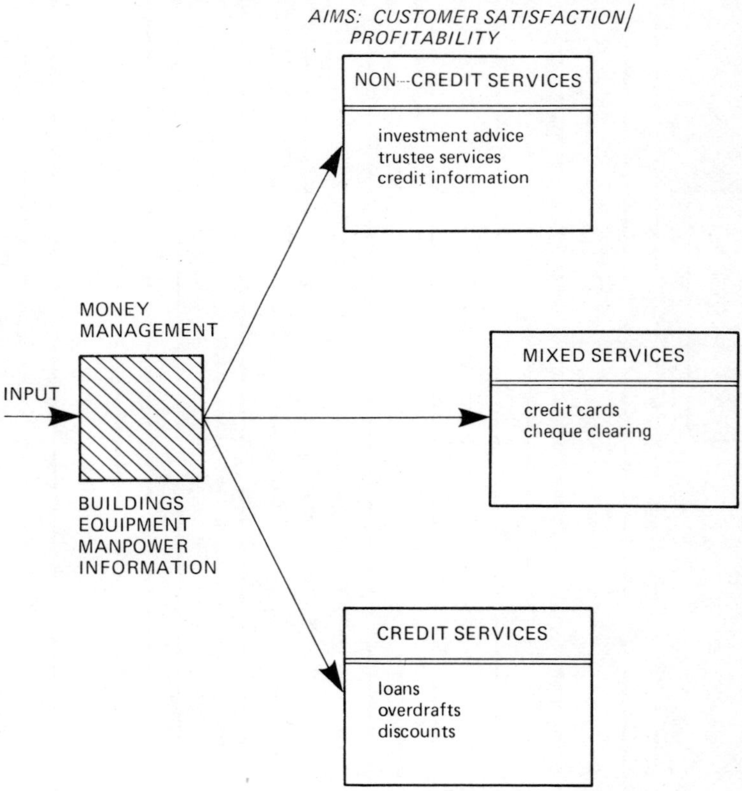

Fig. 2. A bank's output.

distinction between the two types, customers using a credit card system, for example, being able to use the service simply as a means of settling debt or additionally taking advantage of the credit facilities provided.

Figure 2 illustrates schematically these services – the output side of a bank system. These are the corporate objectives and within this broad category main and subsidiary objectives may be distinguished.

BANK OBJECTIVES

One essential function of management in a bank is to take decisions about its output. A bank needs clearly to define its role, to decide what services it is going to provide and which, if any, it is going to develop or alter. The issues involved are often complex, the introduction of a new service, for example, probably having a wide-ranging effect. What, for instance, is likely to be the effect on the cheque-clearing and overdraft services of introducing credit cards? What would be the advantages and disadvantages of providing a new issues service in a commercial bank?

Failure of a system to adjust to changing circumstances can lead to problems and, ultimately, to disaster. A film-making company providing films for the cinema may go out of business if, in the face of TV competition, it fails to redefine its role. Could it include in its output films made for TV advertisers? Or could it redefine its role completely and consider itself a provider of entertainment – start to open bowling alleys and go into Bingo or discotheques?

There have been a number of debates since 1945 about the precise role of a bank. Should the commerical banks confine themselves to the traditional role of short-term lender or should they go in for medium-term lending? Should they take a stake in hire purchase? Should the Trustee Savings Banks introduce a cheque service for their customers?

BANK PROFITS

In defining its functions, a bank's primary aim must be to

increase and maintain its profitability. A bank system has been defined as one which provides a financial service. But a bank is also a system for earning profits. The two views are clearly quite compatible: there is no point in providing a service if nobody wants to buy it and clearly a bank's main objective must be to provide and develop those services which yield a profit consistent with safe business operation and government financial policy.

INPUT AND OUTPUT IN PROFITABLE BALANCE

Figure 3 shows how profit is closely allied to a bank's input and output. Income is generated by the sale of a range of services – output – and this provides the means for paying for inputs into the system – wages and salaries for staff, rent and rates for accommodation and interest on the money deposited with the bank. Any surplus is profit which, after deducting taxation, is ploughed back as reserves or distributed to shareholders as dividends.

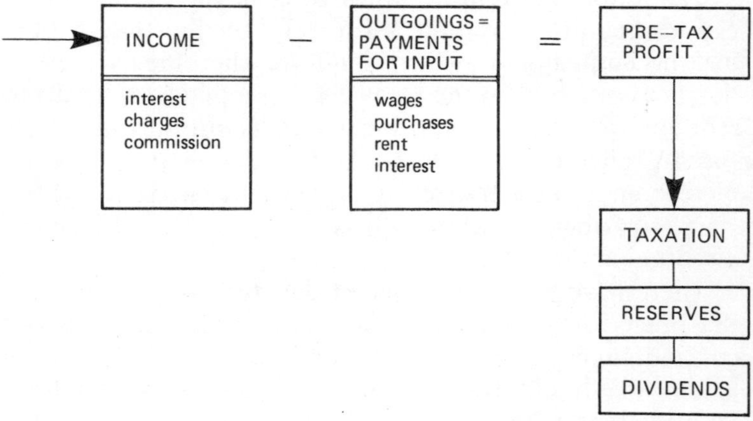

Fig. 3. A bank's profit.

Profitability depends on many factors, not only on the mix of services provided. For example, the cost of inputs has to be taken into account. An important determinant of a bank's profits in the interest differential – the difference between what a bank has to pay for deposits and what it receives as interest for the credit services it provides. In Fig. 3 interest is shown under both income and outgoings and the size of these items is to a large extent determined by the national level of interest rates – high interest rates tending to widen the differential and thus to operate in the bank's favour. To a large extent, this aspect of bank profitability is outside its control and is a good example of the way a bank can only operate as a sub-system within the national economic system.

THE BLACK BOX

Another determinant of profits is the effectiveness of the process which converts a bank's inputs into outputs. The term *black box* is sometimes used to describe this complex process, and can be seen on the left-hand side of Fig. 2; the complexity of the operations it contains can be realised if we think, for example, of all the stages required to turn a deposit of money into a bank loan.

The day-to-day efficiency of the bank, that is the effectiveness of the operations contained within the black box, cannot fail to affect the level of profitability. Inefficient deployment of staff leads to overmanning and inflates the cost of an important input; bad organisation of procedures reduces the level of output below that which could be attained.

WHAT DOES TOP MANAGEMENT DO?

From what has been said it will be seen that the main tasks of top management can be divided into three areas:

1. **Develop Objectives**
   The mix of services forming the bank's output must be what customers want or can be persuaded to want, and what is offered must maximise the bank's profit. Top management must therefore take policy decisions

concerning the bank's role and must establish a suitable development strategy.

2. **Manpower and Input Planning**
If planned output is to be met, the right input must be obtained. This will involve *manpower planning*, that is making sure that an adequate supply of trained staff is available at the right time to provide the services the bank offers now and plans to offer in the future. Decisions must be taken regarding facilities such as premises and computer installations as well as concerning the input of funds, for example, the rates of interest to be offered to depositors and whether and how to increase the bank's permanent capital.

3. **Optimise Use of Resources**
The processes within the black box must be effective – the bank must run efficiently, the optimum use must be made of available resources and the difference in value between inputs and outputs must be maximised.

DOES SIZE AFFECT MANAGEMENT?

In a small organisation, the functions of top management can be carried out quite informally. A small group of men can fairly quickly and easily decide major policy issues. Top management is likely to know most of the staff, to be aware of their capabilities and to be pretty sure of what they are up to most of the time.

In large banks, this is not possible. Conscious efforts have to be made to establish procedures for the effective discharge of the major functions and top management has to decide how it will decide!

How, for example, is it to know *when* to take decisons? Is it going to be content to take action only when major problems arise or will it adopt a positive approach to the decision-taking function and to the effective running of the bank? It may find it necessary to draw on the services of outside consultants for advice on the best organisational structure and may decide to divide the bank into major operational units or divisions. To assist in the management process it may be considered desirable to operate on a *regional* basis through local head offices, and the possibility of establishing local boards of directors will have to be discussed. The role of these units will have to be defined carefully and decisions taken as to the degree of autonomy they are to be permitted to exercise.

In a large organisation, special attention must be paid to the problems of communication. Unless there are effective channels of communication downwards those at levels below top management will not be aware of the bank's policy and their own responsibilities. Equally important are the channels of communication from below. Without a free flow of relevant information there is no real basis for effective decision-taking. *Feed-back mechanisms* need to be established so that the practical working of the bank can be monitored and the practical effectiveness of the decisions taken judged.

HOW TO MAKE A PROFIT?

As stated earlier, a major objective of a bank is to earn satisfactory profits, but this is not a simple objective. There are plenty of examples – current and historical, British and foreign – of banks running into trouble through unsound operations. The main aim of a business enterprise must be to remain in existence. For this, profits must be earned, for no body of shareholders will long accept with equanimity statements by the chairman describing the excellent services the bank is providing, but regretting that there are no profits for distribution. A good profit record is also needed if a bank is seeking to raise new funds in the market, and reserves cannot be built up and the business strengthened if they are not earned.

Although a bank pursuing profit objectives will observe

the spirit as well as the letter of the law, it is likely from time to time to find that there are pressures from both within and from outside to pursue policies not compatible with profit maximisation. A bank may find itself pressed by government to help particular sectors of the economy – exports at one stage, local authorities at another. There may be pressures to help particular industries or other financial institutions. The political and social climate may lead to criticism of certain aspects of bank policy, but a little later the climate may change, the same policy being received with approbation. Where discretion is allowed, the bank will have to decide how far it is to yield to these conflicting pressures; often a compromise has to be found.

Similar decisions may be needed because of internal pressures. A director or influential customer may, for example, urge the bank to pursue a line not conducive to maximum profitability. There may be pressure to provide banking facilities in an unprofitable area, to negotiate an unsatisfactory merger, or to support a particular charitable or educational body.

Often it is difficult to reconcile an efficient personnel policy with maximum profits. Job security for staff is an obvious example, and raises the fundamental question of whether the bank should adopt a hire-and-fire policy or a more paternalistic approach. Staff are frequently recruited at an early age and have security of a tenure for forty years or more. Selecting the winner of the 2.30 is difficult, choosing human material is much more so. Few managers, if they were frank, would claim that their selection procedures were infallible. Also, particulary at a time of rapid change, the bank's requirements alter and the skills of some staff may no longer be required. Granting security of tenure may be justified by arguing that the bank is large enough to absorb everybody without serious effect on its profitability, that such a policy helps to maintain staff morale, curbs demand for higher pay and leads to better staff motivation and loyalty. Equally it may be argued that a few dismissals for incompetence would have salutary effects and help profits.

MANAGEMENT STYLE

By its style, top management will set the image for the whole bank. Is it to be a brash, "go-go", highly-motivated concern or a rather old-fashioned, quiet, slightly fuddy-duddy institution? Where between these extremes will the bank's image rest?

The answer will largely be found in the actions of top management. Will it spend money protecting cashiers from violent attack for reasons that have nothing to do with profits? Will it refuse to vet the wife of an employee being considered for promotion on the grounds that this is uncivilised, unfair and an affront to human dignity? Will it subsidise the sports club and operatic society when this cannot be justified in profit terms?

MANAGEMENT IN A CHANGING WORLD

This introductory chapter has been devoted to a consideration of *corporate planning* – the need to define objectives, decide about the mix of services to be provided and how to achieve the effective and efficient operation of the bank, so as to maximise profits. This theme will be developed in later chapters.

It is also appropriate here to sound a note of warning: a rigid plan, procedures, and methods, can be counter-productive. We live in a world of change and a bank must be alive to the fact that profitable ventures can suddenly appear for which it has no planned response. Great care must therefore be taken to ensure that sufficient flexibility is built into the system so that full advantage may be taken of any opportunities the bank may meet in its uncertain future.

DISCUSSION QUESTIONS

1. "Managers are not the only people who manage." Consider this statement.
2. A system has been described as a grouping of resources for a definite objective. Describe three different types of system and state their objectives.
3. What are the objectives of a bank system?
4. In what way have the objectives of banks changed in the last twenty years?
5. What is the role of profit in a bank system?
6. Why would you expect to find differences between banks in the time and effort devoted to planning?
7. What do you understand by the term "black box"? What is its connection with the level of bank profits?
8. Why should a bank preserve an element of flexibility in its operations?
9. Give three examples of a bank service; a credit service; a non-credit service and a mixed service.
10. "Sound banking is more important than good management." Do you agree?

CHAPTER II

Planning and Control

"...numerous branches required a peculiar mode of government, and a rigid system of discipline. The chief officer of such a bank should be a good banker, and something more. He must be a good administrator...."

J. W. Gilbart

FUNCTIONS OF MANAGEMENT

Bank management has the task of *planning, organising, directing, co-ordinating,* and *controlling* the system for which it is responsible. These are the functions of management.

Little is to be gained from trying to define the term management too precisely, from attempting to draw distinctions between those inside and those outside the management team, from considering how the work of a manager differs from that of a supervisor. It is clear also that the staff grading of a bank employee or the title of a post held is a poor indicator of his management role. For instance, it is quite possible to hold a senior managerial appointment which entails the exercise of considerable technical skill backed up by a wealth of practical experience, but which has no actual management content as defined above. On the other hand, someone occupying a far more junior position may need a good deal of management ability although the necessary technical expertise is much less. We have to be careful with labels: they are dangerous things – the contents of a bottle are always more important than the description on the outside.

LEADERSHIP

A manager has to provide *leadership* and has to control the work of others. He has to ensure that the best results are obtained from his own efforts and from those for whom he is responsible. His responsibilities are likely to grow as he becomes more senior: the higher he goes the more scope there is for involving the bank in loss through wrong decisions or for earning it a larger profit through correct ones.

There are likely also to be temporal and spatial differences in his management role. A junior manager is concerned mainly with the short period, involving himself with the day-to-day problems of his part of the system. Top management needs to take a longer view. The man or woman responsible for a branch or some other section of the bank's work has to make sure the day's tasks are completed, that head office and other returns depart on time, that monthly checking procedures are conducted efficiently. Those at the apex of the management hierarchy should be considering next year's profit prospects and the role of banking at the end of the decade. Whilst those at the very top are concerning themselves with the progress of the bank as a whole, those lower down the line will be thinking only of their part of the system. In other words, the higher the level of management the greater the need to take an overall view of the system and its progress over a longer period of time.

PLANNING

In the last chapter the broad view was taken, looking at a bank system as a whole and the services it provided (Fig. 2). We considered the profitability of a bank system and used Fig. 3 to show how profits are determined by the difference between the income received from the services provided and the payments made for inputs into the system. These inputs are shown in Fig. 4. Staff, buildings, equipment and other facilities are needed to provide bank

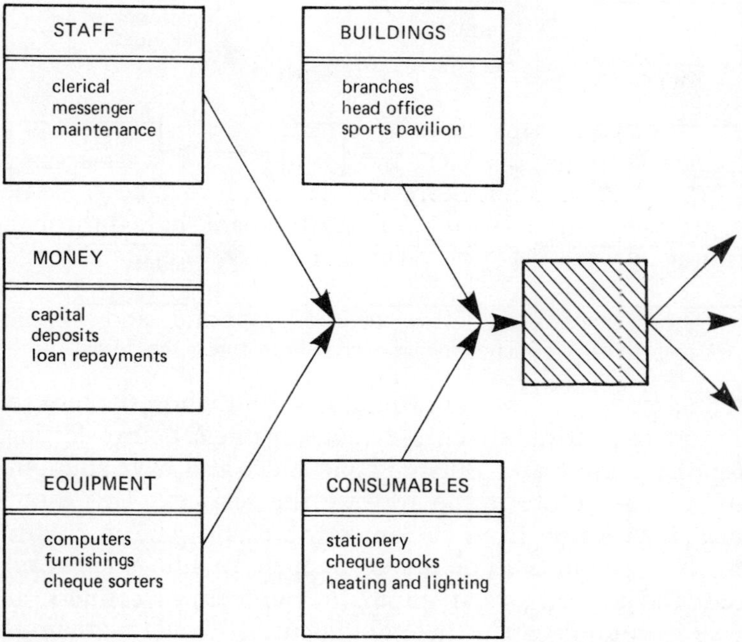

Fig. 4. **How a bank's inputs combine to provide a satisfactory service.**

services, and the whole complex of operations required to turn inputs into outputs is shown in the black box on the right.

A complete bank system is depicted in Fig. 5. The inputs of Fig. 4 are combined with the outputs of Fig. 2. The black box now appears in the centre and provides the vital link between the resources used by the bank and the services it provides for its customers.

The complete bank system shown in Fig. 5 is deceptively simple, particularly with the use of the black box to show what goes on inside a bank. Suppose that the bank is going to lend a customer £1,000, the output in this case being in the form of a credit service. Elements from all five categories of input will be needed. The customer may ask for a secured advance when he calls to see his branch manager (a staff input) who is likely to be seated at a desk

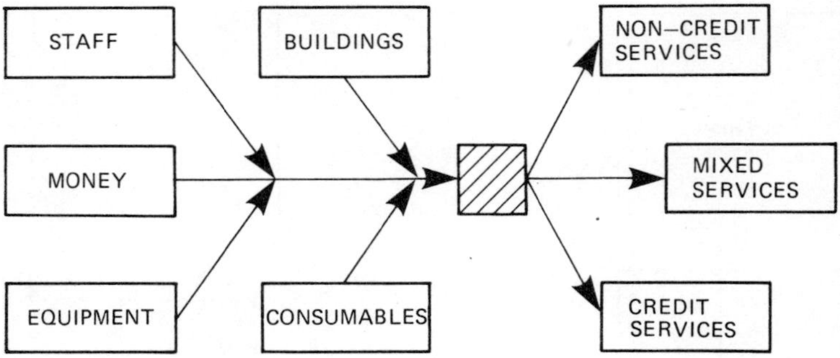

Fig. 5. A bank system combining inputs and outputs in the "black box".

(equipment) in his room (buildings) and who asks him to complete a form of charge (consumables) before letting him have the loan. But the bank must also have an input of money before it can provide the service. This input may have come from customers who have paid in credits to their accounts. For this to happen, buildings are again required as well as staff inputs in the form of cashiers, as well as counters and other equipment. It would be tedious to continue, but obviously recording the transactions and clearing the cheques will involve other staff, as well as more stationery and items of equipment such as computers and cheque sorters.

The role of top management is considered on p. 7; there are three main tasks – concerned with the bank's output, its input and the processes taking place within the black box. But of course top management might not agree. It might sit back and do nothing. It might take the view that the system was working perfectly well, that most people seemed content and that the shareholders were happy with the level of profit the system was generating. Experienced, competent staff might be doing a good job looking after the bank's international and domestic operations whilst those responsible for premises, staff and equipment might be handling day-to-day problems efficiently. As senior bankers they might feel that considering large advance applications, meeting important customers, interpreting government policy and attending staff functions was their proper role which provided them with an arduous and exhausting working day with no more time for other things.

Under these circumstances, top management could hardly be said to be managing: members of the team would not be involved in planning, organising, directing, co-ordinating and controlling the system. With reasonable luck they might safely reach honourable retirement and some might eventually come to occupy a seat on the Board. One can imagine a series of retirement parties at which the Chairman, witty and urbane as always, would outline a career pattern which commenced more than forty years ago with the waste at Little Puddlecombe-on-Sea. Younger men might be enjoined to emulate the skills of the departing and there might be talk of shrewd bankers adept at detecting a possible bad debt or a shaky security.

But things could go wrong – or at best not turn out as well as they might have done if there had been good management. A competitor might introduce a new service which proved extremely popular, with the result that there is a serious drain of good accounts. Lack of co-ordination might mean that the supply and training of staff proved inadequate for the changed needs of the system. It might be found that the computer facilities no longer provided the desired service, that buildings or equipment were inadequate or that the domestic or overseas branch network was not suitable for modern purposes. Had the future been more carefully planned, more sensitive targets and standards set up, this situation might well have been avoided.

THE CORPORATE PLAN

Without some form of corporate plan a bank system cannot be properly managed, for without it objectives cannot be defined nor the strategy devised for achieving them.

FORMAL OR INFORMAL PLAN?

The plan can take many forms. In a small bank, it may be carried in the heads of one or two men who have agreed implicitly or explicitly what they are trying to do and how they plan to do it. In a large bank, it can be a very lengthy and detailed document, prepared by top executives in consultation with senior staff and approved by the board of directors. Much will depend on the bank's attitude to planning, on its experience of the planning process and on its willingness to devote resources of time and effort to the work.

LONG-TERM OBJECTIVES

The importance of defining the bank's role was explained on p. 5 and the plan might well start by considering the future from this point of view. An attempt might be made to consider the part the bank will be playing in the country's financial system in ten or more years' time, taking into account likely changes in the size and distribution of personal and corporate incomes, changing international trade patterns and changes in the social framework within which the bank operates.

MEDIUM-TERM NEEDS

The plan might turn then to the immediate future and consider what profit growth it should seek to achieve in, say, the next five years, whether it can reasonably aim to increase profits sufficiently to preserve the purchasing power of the shareholders' dividends during a period of inflation or whether it can be more optimistic and seek to increase the real return to shareholders. It might consider its reserve position and the level of profits needed to allow it to plough back the necessary funds or it might consider its rating on the Stock Exchange, knowing that shortly it will need to raise additional permanent capital. Realistic attempts could be made to forecast balance sheet variables, the level of advances that might be attained and the amount of new deposits that might be attracted. It could consider suggestions that its share of total deposits might be increased, it might estimate income growth from its various services and outline possible action to ensure that its profit targets were reasonable when considered in the light of current information.

COSTING

Quite clearly no meaningful plan can be established without the fullest possible information. An efficient *costing system* is needed so that the cost of different services and of running different parts of the system can be established as precisely as possible. The bank needs to be able to distinguish profitable services from less profitable ones and to know which, if any, are making losses. A few years ago, for example, a major bank estimated that the cost of a manager's time amounted to £6 an hour, clearly a most useful piece of information when deciding on the scope of bank advisory services. Collecting such information costs money but the real value of a corporate plan depends upon the amount and quality of the information on which it is based. Management must decide what costs it is prepared to incur in the planning process.

But a corporate plan should not confine itself to purely financial matters. As well as establishing growth targets for profits, deposits and other aggregates and establishing a policy for various bank services, it can deal with innumerable other aspects of the bank's work. One section of the plan might deal with staffing, for example with recruitment and training. It may be decided that steps will be taken to reduce staff turnover, to re-orientate staff training programmes so that more emphasis is placed on the marketing of bank services. Changes may be sought in the quality of staff joining the bank; a higher or lower proportion of graduate intake may be planned or changes may be introduced regarding C.S.E. and G.C.E. examination passes needed by certain grades of staff. Plans may be set out dealing with changes in the bank's computing arrangements, with the modernisation and improvement of bank premises or with procurement procedures for bank stationery. Plans for major organisational changes can be introduced leading, for example, to more or less decentralisation. In turn, this could lead to major changes of policy concerning, for example, the method of charging customers' securities.

CONTROL

A proper planning strategy means that management is forced to consider the system for which it is responsible. Strategic plans can be established to achieve objectives and individuals can be shown more clearly what is expected of them. Better co-ordination is possible and bottlenecks can be avoided. Staff can be recruited and trained ready to operate a new service; if a service is to be phased out, plans can be laid for the redeployment of staff.

There are disadvantages, too. Apart from the cost of planning in time and effort, factors beyond the bank's control can quickly make a plan obsolete. A change in government monetary or fiscal policy, action by a competitor or an overseas government can mean that targets are no longer attainable, or that new fields for action and profit are suddenly opened up. Plans need to be frequently revised in the light of new information, and failure to do so is likely to increase the dangers of inflexibility mentioned at the end of the last chapter.

Proper planning represents a scientific approach to bank management. Progress may be monitored by comparing what actually happens with what was planned and the appearance of unfavourable trends can more quickly be discerned. Management gains increased control over the bank system and, properly conceived and executed, the planning process has a salutary effect on staff, partly by increasing their interest in what is going on and partly by forcing them to reconsider their functional role and the contribution they can make to the effective operation of the system as a whole.

LOOK AT THE TIME SCALE

Great advantages accrue when the corporate plan is analysed on a time and functional basis. Thus, a planned profit increase of 30 per cent over a five-year period implies a cumulative profit growth of about 5 per cent a year. In the strategic planning process the contribution of different parts of the system to this annual growth figure is considered and it may be found, for example, that the growth potential from international operations is greater than in the domestic field. Likewise it may appear that some areas of the country have a better potential than others, so that a bank with a large branch network can set different growth targets for its various regions. Things can be arranged so that each region can have what is in effect its own mini-plan which outlines the region's future and establishes various targets on an annual basis. Where this is the case, the ideal situation is for plans to be drawn up for the region and then incorporated in the overall plan, those in charge of the region having an opportunity of commenting on the final version. This "participation" is now a recognised feature of modern planning and control systems.

In these circumstances, each region knows what is expected of it during the following year, what contribution to profit growth is looked for and how this is to be accomplished. Targets can be set for the growth of deposits and advances and for other aspects of the region's work such as staffing and premises, or the development of various services. The regional plan might, for instance, say that the growth of deposits and advances is to be achieved without increasing staff, or that additional staff will only be available to run a particular service. The precise form of the plan will be determined by the bank and to some extent will depend on the degree of autonomy enjoyed by the region. If responsibility for premises is centralised, the plan may not mention the subject. Again, where the provision of a service is the responsibility of a central agency, detailed plans for the service may be established for that agency with the plans for a region containing only matters which concern them; for example, a statement saying that branches should discourage the use of the service.

MONITORING PROGRESS

Where individual plans are developed for regions, for departments and for different aspects of a bank's work, close control of the system is possible. Performance indicators or targets may provide a yardstick against which performance can be measured. If a region exceeds its profit target by a substantial margin, the cause can be investigated. If it can be shown that the good performance is the result of hard work and efficiency, this can be recognised at the next round of salary increases. If particular methods have been adopted to achieve good results, it might be possible to introduce these methods in other regions. If extraneous and unexpected factors are the cause, these might be investigated and appropriate amendments made in due course to the regional plan as well as to the bank's corporate plan.

This ability to monitor progress is very important. It might be found in one region that there has been a sudden reduction in demand for a particular service which investigation shows is likely to spread to other regions. As a result it might prove possible to take remedial action throughout the country, possibly by a change in the advertising programme. By comparing progress of different regions, unsuspected changes in the country's economic and social pattern may be discovered thus enabling the bank to be prepared and thus to improve its operational efficiency.

On the input side, it will be important to develop flexible budgetary control; this must be linked with the output if revenue and costs are to be realistically matched.

DISCUSSION QUESTIONS

1. Why does sound planning involve also an efficient costing system?
2. Attempting to plan future profits is a waste of time, there are too many unknown factors involved. Do you agree?
3. Why should a corporate plan not confine itself simply to financial matters? What non-financial matters would you expect to find in a corporate plan?
4. Is it possible to hold a senior managerial appointment without being a manager?
5. Why is it important for a bank to define its role?
6. What are the advantages of analysing a corporate plan on a time and functional basis?
7. Describe the direct and indirect advantages of a sound system for monitoring progress.
8. What factors determine the amount of time and effort devoted by a bank to the planning process?
9. What are the main inputs to a bank system?
10. A large bank faces problems which do not apply to small banks. What are they?

CHAPTER III

Line Management

"Those bankers who extend their commands to the minutest details of the office, exacting the most rigid obedience in matters the most trivial, harshly censuring their clerks when they do wrong, and never commending them when they do right, may themselves be very clever men, but they do not go the way to get clever assistants."

J. W. Gilbart

BREAKING DOWN THE CORPORATE PLAN

Management is not a science*, but there is no doubt that efficient bank management in the twentieth century requires a systematic approach to the operation and development of a bank system. Corporate planning exemplifies this approach: people think about where they are going and how they propose to get there.

By breaking down the corporate plan to cover various parts of the system, those responsible for different aspects of the bank's work are required to consider:

1. their role,
2. their contribution to the system,
3. methods to be used to attain their objectives.

Quite clearly they do not need to know every detail of the corporate plan. An executive responsible for a group of domestic branches is unlikely to be affected by plans

* F. W. Taylor was the father of the so-called "scientific management" movement. However, he was concerned with the application of scientific method to the collection and use of information in order to improve efficiency; this does not of itself constitute a "science". On the other hand the social sciences do play an important part in the study and application of management.

concerned with overseas operations. Indeed to flood him with a mass of paper full of irrelevant information is likely to prove counterproductive. Clearly, too, there are aspects of planning which must be regarded as secret. No bank is likely to be very pleased if there is a leak of information, the financial press carrying an article giving the bank's profit target for the year and comparing it with the actual results. Likewise plans to acquire shares in a financial house or to merge with another institution are unlikely to appear in writing and may remain the closely guarded secret of a very limited number of people, possibly only of the chairman and chief executive.

THE OPERATIONAL PLAN

The aim should be to provide every manager with an agreed operational plan containing sufficient information for his needs. As Viscount Montgomery put it in his memoirs:

> "I did not always tell *all* the truth to the soldiers in the war . . . . I told them all they must know for the efficient carrying out of their tasks."

The number and nature of these plans is likely to vary considerably, to a large extent depending on the size and complexity of the bank system and on the attitude of management to planning and control. There will clearly be considerable differences in plans concerning domestic and international business and again between these and plans for departments concerned with staffing or premises or for those dealing with major bank services such as trustee work, taxation or investment. The amount of detail contained in planning documents will also vary, the corporate plan for a large bank with a widespread domestic branch network making no attempt to deal with individual branches. Plans would in this case be established on a regional basis, each executive responsible for a region dealing with more detailed planning in his own area.

How this will operate as far as individual branches are concerned will again depend on bank attitudes as well as those of executives with regional responsibilities.

BRANCH MANAGEMENT

Planning is not exclusive to the "boys at the top", to the chief executive, to heads of large divisions and departments or to regional executives. There is a planning element in most people's work. Girls in the typing pool, unless strictly regimented, may have some choice in the way they plan the day's work; staff dealing with credits in an overseas department may have even more freedom. A good worker is usually one who plans his work properly, has clear objectives and proceeds systematically towards achieving them. This is especially true of a good branch manager.

Consider the following hypothetical case histories of two men both starting to manage a branch for the first time.

CASE STUDY 1

Jack Roberts bade farewell to his old branch on Friday and took up his new post on the following Monday morning. He was well-prepared for his new job. He had served in a number of branches, was technically competent and well aware of a branch manager's duties, indeed he took charge of his old branch for three months when the manager was ill and received a very complimentary letter from Head Office as a result. Soon after he joined the new branch he went along to meet the regional manager, who proved to be very friendly, assured him of his full support and told him not to hesitate to call on him for advice if he needed it.

He ran his new branch well. Deposits showed a small but steady increase, the number of accounts rose and his lending was sound. His return of bad and doubtful debts raised no problems, all his secured advances were properly charged. Head Office was pleased and a few years later he received his second managership. He left the routine running of the branch to his deputy, concentrating his main efforts on interviewing customers with whom he rapidly developed good relations. When he returned their hospitality they found him an urbane and pleasant host. But he never liked to be away from the branch for too long. He regarded himself as a shrewd and successful banker, believed in keeping a keen eye on what was going on in the branch and was never greatly impressed with the stories he heard of modern "go-go" methods. All returns to Head Office had to pass his keen eye, he personally ensured that securities were properly charged, made sure he saw the documents handled by his foreign exchange clerk and was meticulous when carrying out routine checking duties.

CASE STUDY 2

At about the same time, John Smith took over the management of his new branch. He was technically as efficient as Roberts and his career had followed a similar pattern. But he approached his first managerial appointment in a rather different way. He decided to put to good use the few weeks left before he took up his new appointment. He telephoned the manager whom he was to succeed and arranged to visit him, making a mental note that when he took over he would have to do something about the way in which the telephone was answered. Before the visit he spent a Sunday afternoon looking around the area where he was to operate, noting some of its important features: a large hospital, one of the new Polytechnics in the process of building new student accommodation and two shopping centres, one consisting mainly of large multiples, the other, much smaller, but with a block of four new shops in course of erection, made up wholly of one-man businesses. He noted with interest a large triangular site with many old buildings and indications that the demolition gangs were about to move in.

His first visit to the new branch went well. The manager introduced him to senior members of the staff and gave him details of the main accounts, mentioning the names of those he was taking with him. He had no information about the site where demolition was about to start, but he agreed to return after Smith had taken over, to have lunch with him and to introduce him to some of the more important customers.

Before taking up his new appointment, Smith was able to visit the local planning department from whom he learned that planning permission had been granted for a sixteen-storey office block to be built on the site where demolition was taking place. He was interested in the names of the developers who were large borrowers from the bank and he wondered whether it would be possible for them to let the bank have early details of lettings so that he could approach tenants about their banking requirements before they moved into occupation. Clearly he would have to telephone the manager of the developers' branch as soon as possible to see what could be done.

He arranged another visit, this time to his new regional manager who greeted him in much the same way as he had greeted Roberts. Smith asked him whether plans were available for the development of business in the region and where his new branch fitted into the picture. It appeared that no specific plans had been prepared and no profit targets established. However, the regional manager told him that recently there had been a meeting of local managers attended by two general managers and the bank's policy had been discussed. What had emerged was that under current restrictions little could be done to expand advances, but that the bank was particularly interested in increasing deposits and selling the bank's new services, in particular the new computer services for customers being developed by the bank's subsidiary.

THE MANAGEMENT APPROACH

The story of our two fictional characters is worth

careful consideration. Although Smith's approach was different from that of Roberts' there is nothing to show that he was a worse banker. There is no reason why his lending record should not be as good as Roberts', why the branch should be less efficient or why he should not be as highly regarded by customers. As far as we know he *is* as good a banker as Roberts, but he has brought something extra to his first managership. In a just world he would have been promoted at least as quickly as Roberts and some would say that his approach marked him out as a man, who, with more experience, would make an admirable replacement for the regional manager.

But we don't know anything about Smith's progress and it would probably be as well not to be too optimistic. There are indications that the bank is not very interested in planning. No plans had been established for the region and all Smith was able to find out about bank policy was that it was anxious to expand deposits and sell its new computer service. Although pleasant, the regional manager was not very helpful. He gave Roberts no help at all and Smith had to take the initiative and seek guidance. If the regional manager had been adopting a management approach we would have expected him to outline plans for the region to both men, indicate what they could do to help and what their aims should be. He seems to have regarded it as no part of his job to indicate what staffing and other problems they would face in running their first branch or to give them any indication of the scope for development in their new area.

The result was that Smith took over his branch with a number of objectives which he had discovered but with no clear idea of what specific targets he was expected to meet. One of his first tasks therefore was to discuss objectives with his deputy. They agreed that it should be possible to obtain fifty new accounts during the next ten months, that there was no point in taking accounts from other branches and that they would try and obtain business either from those who had no bank account or from customers of other banks. It was agreed that their main effort would be to obtain credit balances, but that they would not worry too much about the size of account. Smith pointed out that an average balance on the new accounts of £100 would represent an increase in branch deposits of about 4 per cent. His deputy expressed concern about the additional cost to the bank of servicing these accounts but Smith told him that bank policy was to increase deposits and that there had been no indication that account was to be taken of the costs of achieving this growth.

It was agreed that the Polytechnic, with an intake of perhaps 750 new students a year, was an attractive target for new business although average balances on these accounts were likely to be small. It was recognised also that the hospital might be a source of new business although its main potential might be as a purchaser of the new computer service. Neither Smith or his deputy knew much about hospital administration, but one of the senior administrative staff had been a customer of the branch for many years and Smith made up his mind to take an early opportunity of talking to him. The proposed office block, due for completion within two years, was clearly a good potential market and although little immediate action was possible Smith said he would pursue his idea of trying to obtain the names of future tenants.

Although we shall never know how the bank or Smith benefited from his efforts, we can at least see that he was trying to adopt a management approach to his new job, taking an early opportunity of formulating objectives and developing a strategy to attain them.

DISCUSSION QUESTIONS

1. "There is a planning element in most people's work." Explain.
2. What should be the role of the branch manager in the 1970s?

3. What aspects of your bank's corporate plan do you need to know in order to do your present job efficiently and effectively?
4. Draw up a five-year plan for your branch or office.
5. To what extent should a branch manager be involved in the establishment of a corporate plan for a large bank?
6. "A young banker should concentrate on becoming technically efficient and not waste time learning about management." Consider and critically discuss this statement.
7. What steps would you take to prepare youself for taking over the managership of the branch where you are already deputy manager.
8. What is the role of regional management in the planning process?
9. How much time should a manager spend talking to junior staff in his branch?
10. What sources of information could you use to discover future building development in your area?
11. Discuss the two outline case studies and reach conclusions on the likely outcome of the two different approaches.

CHAPTER IV

Communicating Information

"...place near together those clerks whose duties will require them to have frequent communication with each other."

J. W. Gilbart

HARMONY OF OBJECTIVES

Smith, adopting a management approach to his new job, provided himself with targets to aim at and a development strategy to help him achieve results. One target was to open an average of five accounts a month and the strategy involved the hospital, future tenants in the office block and the local Polytechnic. As we have seen, he had already started to consider the tactics he would employ, for example, by planning to have a talk with one of the hospital administrators.

As far as he could judge, the plans seemed to be in line with bank policy, but he had not had much to go on and what he had discovered had been through his own initiative. His task would have been easier if the bank had developed better information and communication facilities.

A SYSTEM'S NEEDS

All systems depend for their effective operation on communication and information. The human body constantly receives information through its sensory system which enables it to survive: if someone has a headache he goes to the medicine chest. A manufacturing company depends for its survival and efficiency on up-to-date information about the state of its order book and its current stock levels of raw materials and finished goods. It runs into trouble if the information is defective or if channels of communication are partially blocked or non-existent.

The information needed by a system is generated both internally and externally. Internal information tells a human being when he needs food and drink, external information warns him when he is about to bump into a wall. Smith sought information internally from the regional manager and his predecessor and externally from the local planning authority and by touring the area where he was to work. This need for information is required also by those in charge of the system as a whole. We have seen (p.19) that the value of a corporate plan depends largely on the quantity and quality of the information upon which it is based and that a bank should start by considering the changing economic, political and social climate in which it operates (p.18). An assessment will be needed of changes taking place in the regional and national economy and, where necessary, of international changes. For example, in planning the pattern of international business some assessment will be needed of the relative growth rates expected in different countries. Political changes indicating, for example, that bank nationalisation is likely may change plans for profit growth or the strategy to be adopted with commission charges. Social changes, such as improvements in the pay and conditions of women, may encourage the bank to plan services geared particulary to their needs.

As may be seen from Fig. 6, two other main areas of external information may be distinguished, those concerned with *technical matters* and those covering the affairs of *competitors*. The bank must take account in its planning of changes taking place in financial markets. Developments in consumer finance are obviously crucial

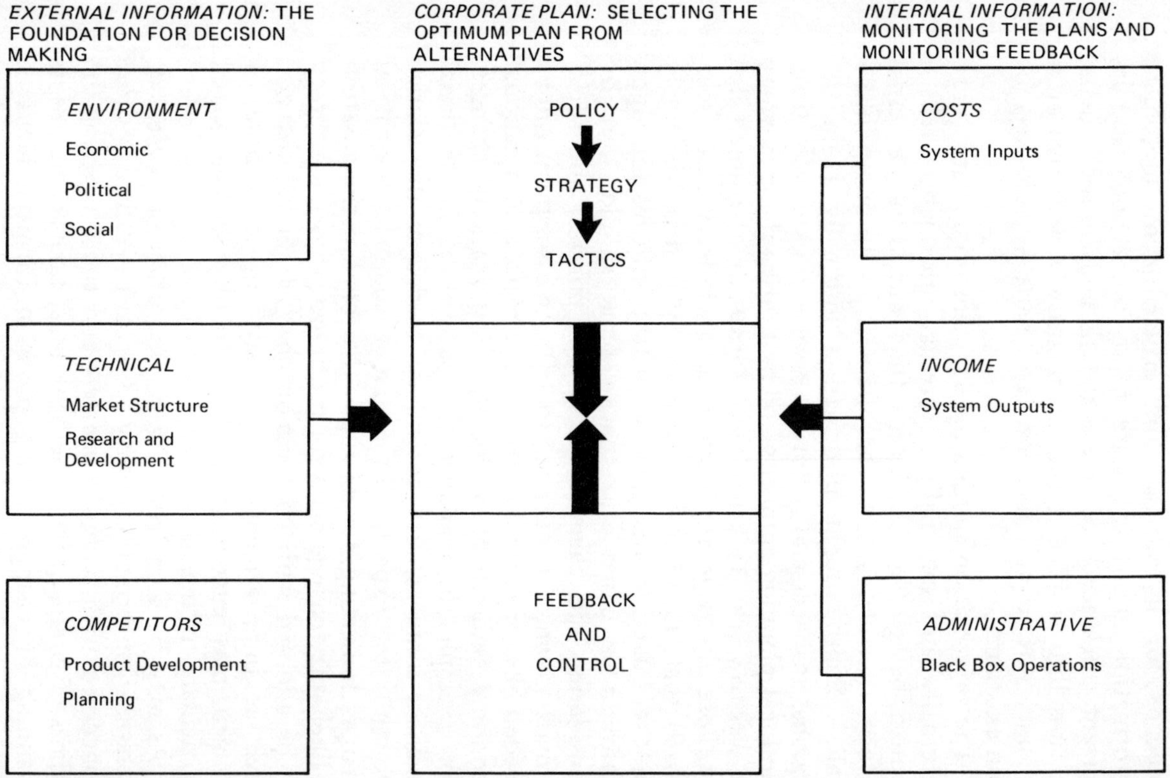

Fig. 6. Planning information.

and it will keep a close watch therefore on what is happening with hire purchase and credit sales business. It will be interested in such things as non-bank personal loan schemes, developments in connection with second mortgages, unit trusts and insurance as well as in aspects of local authority finance. The growth of multi-national corporations, the effects of company mergers, the introduction of certificates of deposit and developments in the Eurocurrency and Eurobond markets are other examples of things about which the bank needs up-to-date information. It also has to keep abreast of technical changes – developments in the computing field, new equipment likely to affect routine work such as the transmission and cash handling services or new thinking on staff training methods.

The third main information source is concerned with the bank's competitors. Rumours that a new service is about to be introduced may cause the bank to reassess its plans and introduce changes of policy. Any information that can be gleaned about the pattern of competitors' costs or their income flows is important, as is news of changes being introduced into their methods of organisation or operation. Quite clearly a bank will wish, too, to keep a close watch on the progress of competitors. Figures published monthly or annually will enable comparisons to be made with movements in the bank's own figures for deposits, advances, investments and reserve assets. Assessing these movements and changes in the profit figures of other banks can provide a useful insight into how policy should be changed, published information being supplemented by that received through formal channels (*e.g.* inter-bank staff meetings at various levels) and informal ones. The development of industrial and commercial espionage using bugging devices, for example, illustrates the importance placed by some organisations on information about their competitors, but it is of course not suggested that British banks should adopt these tactics.

INTERNAL INFORMATION

A bank does not work in a vacuum. It needs to know as much as possible about what is going on outside and to receive an adequate flow of information. This necessarily impinges on the planning process, in particular on the formulation of policy, the development of strategy and the consideration of tactics. But the planning process also includes feedback and control processes and a flow of internal information is needed if these are to be effective.

The importance of an adequate information flow can be seen when we consider more closely the methods of controlling a bank. A measure of the effectiveness of a bank system is the level of profits it generates. It follows that the corporate plan should specify a profit target, using as its measure the return on capital employed (ROCE).

RETURN ON CAPITAL

In measuring progress, this is the crucial indicator to watch. As a business grows, those responsible for its progress will wish to apply the measure to different parts of the system. Firmer control can be exercised and it is possible to compare the progress being made by different units. If, for example, a firm is producing two products, one in a factory in Scotland and the other at plants in the Midlands, it is easy to operate them as autonomous units, as largely independent businesses, each with a measurable return on capital employed. The small central organisation needed to co-ordinate their work and to determine overall company policy will probably have low costs which can easily be allocated to the two operating units or *profit centres*. Control is then exercised by monitoring the progress of these centres.

In practice, particularly in the case of a large bank providing a wide range of inter-related services, the problem of control is not so easy. It may be difficult to delegate authority from the centre and thereby grant a large amount of autonomy to operating units. The profitability of different branches cannot easily be compared, and what about the costs of head office departments? Is it meaningful to compare the return on capital of a branch which has expanded into new expensive freehold property with one that is housed on a long lease at a low fixed rental?

It may therefore be necessary to think in terms of *responsibility centres* rather than profit centres, the planning and control process operating through costs and output and not through return on capital employed. The progress of bank branches may be monitored by measuring changes in staff expenses, the level of deposits and advances, commission and interest income as well as non-financial items such as the number of credits received or cheques cleared.

Important parts of a bank system do not generate income, obvious examples being those concerned with premises and staff. Departments of this type may be regarded as *cost centres*, their effectiveness being measured by the costs incurred in providing an agreed level of service. The notion of profit, responsibility and cost centres can be helpful when deciding what information needs to be collected for an efficient planning and control system. However, rigid distinctions between categories will often be impossible. Some departments provide a service both for customers and for internal use and they thus have the attributes both of cost and profit centres. A system of *internal pricing* could be adopted, other departments being charged for the services they consume, but in practice this may not be worthwhile because of the problems involved in deciding how internal prices are to be determined.

It is therefore clear that if control is to be effective, the main aim of a bank should be to identify *budget centres* and to consider the best means of measuring their activities, whether as profit centres, responsibility centres or cost centres. A large bank may well find that only the major operating units – domestic or international divisions – can be treated fully as profit centres.

BUDGETARY CONTROL

A budget centre, of whatever type, is some part of the bank system for which a separate budget is prepared. These budgets should be drawn up as part of the integrated plan for the bank. They may be regarded as *statements of expected performance and costs for a future period* and serve to define areas of responsibility and the targets to be achieved. Budgets are usually framed in financial terms, money being used as the common measuring rod. This does not mean that non-financial factors are ignored. Thus staffing targets established for different regions of a bank may be translated into financial terms by applying figures for staff pay and other benefits, such as pensions, to the number of staff involved. Again, in establishing a budget for premises, plans for extensions, alterations and maintenance can be shown on a cost basis, the manager responsible for this function having a budget to work within, up to a prescribed expenditure limit.

Establishing budgets in this way is an important part of the internal information flow. They are working documents for parts of the system and communicate to each budget centre what is expected of it. They are also important parts of the planning process and provide feedback – a flow of information from the budget centre to those responsible for the system as a whole – as well as control. The result of actual operations is fed back and measured against the appropriate budget. Deviations or *variances* from what was planned can be investigated and remedial action taken. *Variance analysis* provides a flow of information which enables the system to be monitored and which stimulates action at all levels. Thus, the head of a premises department may establish budgets for the regions under his control, each budget being broken down into the various activities performed there. Regular returns from each region enable the premises manager to discern quickly important variances and to investigate them with the head of region concerned. Likewise these regional heads can see what is happening under each category of activity for which they are responsible, and can take any necessary action if things begin to go wrong.

WHY COMMUNICATE?

An important aspect of budgetary control is that it formalises the upward and downward flow of information in an organisation. In the absence of such flow, proper control is impossible.

Smith, it will be remembered, attempted (in a rudimentary way) to formulate a policy and strategy for his branch. His story indicates that the bank had paid little attention to modern management methods: there was no corporate plan, no budgets, no targets and no indication that anybody had heard of a profit or cost centre. However, Smith – given the time and interest – might have developed his own information-communication-control system. Let us take a simple example: His plan to open fifty new accounts in the first ten months. Section A of Fig. 7 shows his target – an average of five accounts a month – covering the ten-month period to October (we have assumed that his target thereafter remains unaltered) and a record of the actual number of accounts opened in each month. This very simple *bar chart* illustrates one way in which information can be communicated. By comparing the number of current accounts opened with the target figure, he is able to monitor progress and, if he wishes, to take remedial action. Smith has established a simple control system and a record of internal information readily communicated by means of a chart.

CHARTS AND DIAGRAMS

Useful insights may be gained when information is presented in this way. Thus there is evidence from the chart's hypothetical figures that it becomes more difficult

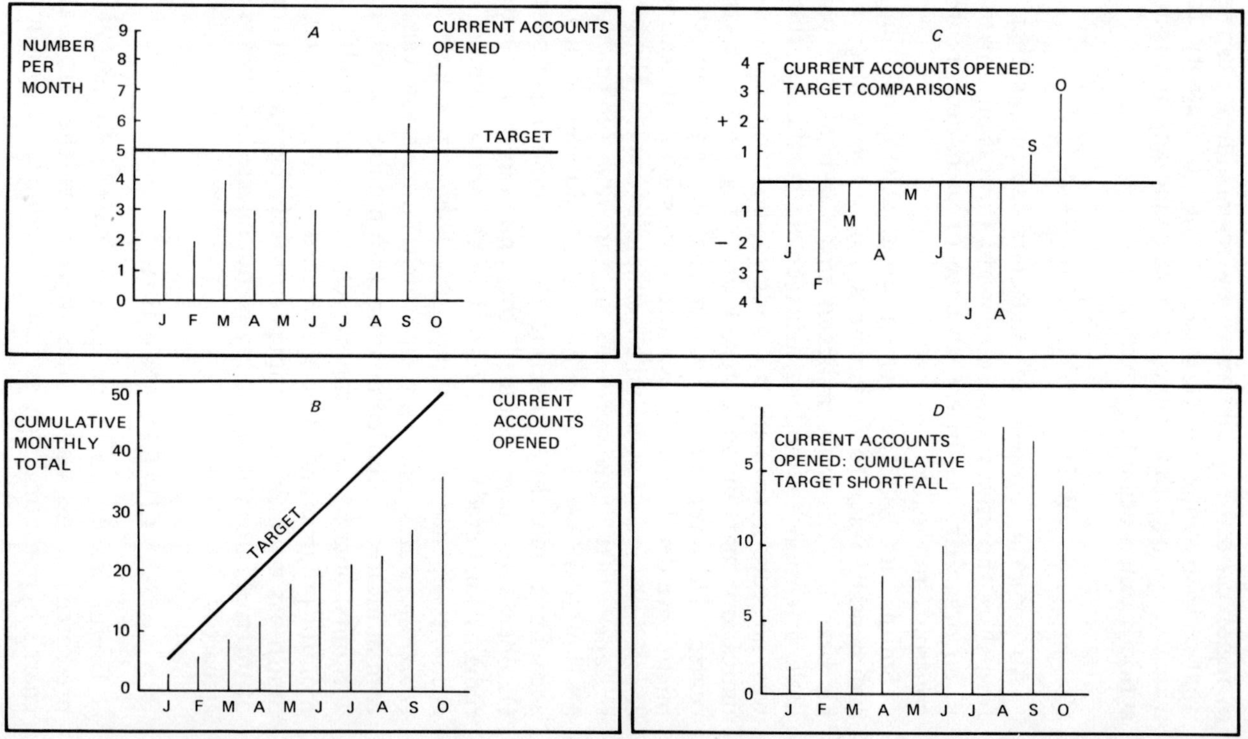

Fig. 7. Communicating progress.

to obtain new accounts in the summer months but that things become easier in the autumn, possibly the result of the new student intake to the local Polytechnic. Comparison with earlier years would be interesting. If this shows that annual patterns are similar it might be sensible to have a target which varies from month to month, or, possibly, a target based on the number of accounts opened in the same month of the previous year.

Figure 7 shows several ways of presenting the same information. In Section B cumulative monthly figures are used. The target rises during progress through the ten-month period, by February, ten accounts should have been opened, by March fifteen. This chart brings out clearly the fact that not only are monthly target figures not being reached, but that the position is worsening through time. Section C shows variances from target, the bars this time signifying for each month the amount by which the number of accounts gained fell short of, or exceeded the planned increase. Finally, in Section D, these variances are added month by month to give the cumulative shortfall. After six months of the planning period the shortfall had risen to ten accounts – only twenty accounts compared with a target of thirty had been opened – and the shortfall continued to rise until September and October when the monthly target was exceeded.

Figure 7 shows clearly how visual presentation of statistical data can be an effective form of communication. A good chart or diagram enables salient features to leap to the eye, but it should be kept as simple as possible and care must be taken that it is not misleading.

Figure 8 illustrates other methods of communication, this time using published figures for deposits of the London Clearing Banks. Section A is a *pie diagram*, used here to bring out clearly how deposits are shared between the five institutions. A circle is drawn and the 360° it contains are then shared proportionally between constituents of the total. Midland had 20 per cent of the deposits at the time the diagram was drawn and thus is

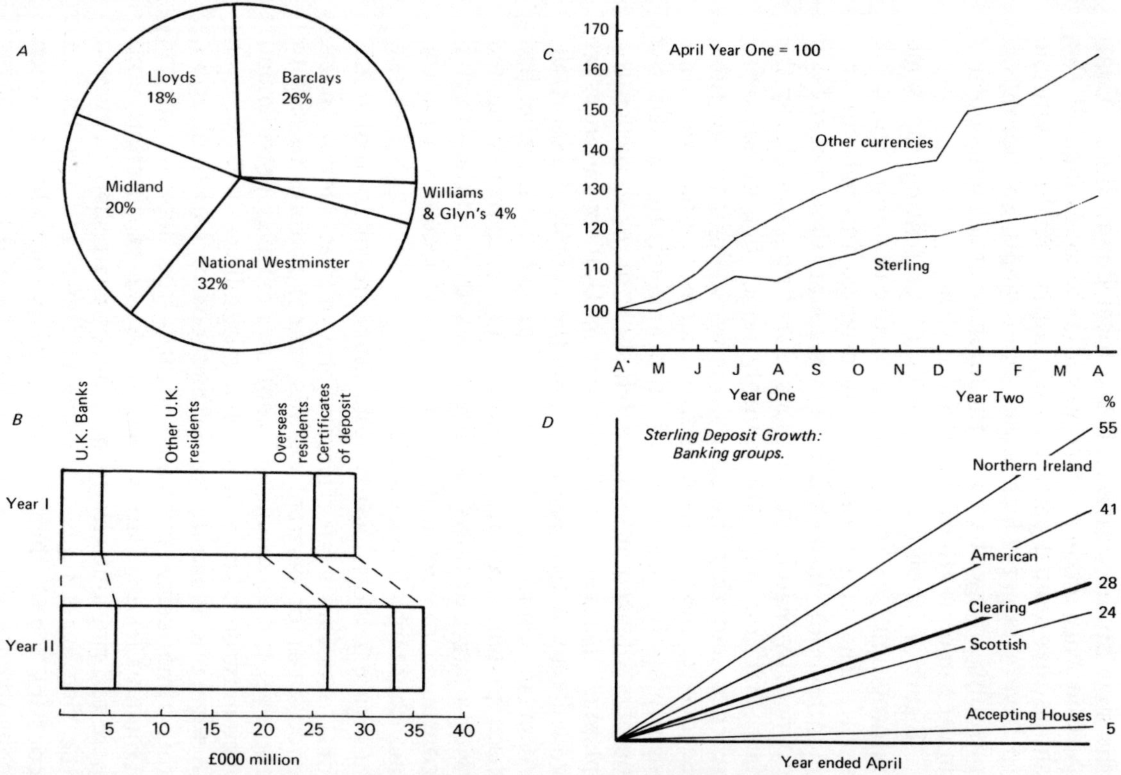

Fig. 8. Communicating information: clearing bank deposits; market shares; sources of deposits; sterling and other deposits; growth rate of deposits.

allocated 20 per cent of the circle, that is 20 per cent of 360° or 72°. In Section B, a similar principle is applied, this time by the subdivision of rectangles. In the example this has been done for two consecutive years and we can see how total deposits have increased over time, how in both years the largest proportion of deposits comes from non-bank U.K. residents and how deposit growth has been derived from three out of the four categories shown. The diagram also shows that Certificates of Deposit shrank between the two years, not only in total but also as a proportion of the whole.

Section C of Fig. 8 shows by means of graphs the share of deposits in sterling and in other currencies. Because of big differences in the figures – sterling deposits in April of Year One amounted to nearly £16,500m whilst other currency deposits were under £1,500m – it is difficult to show them on the same scale. One method of dealing with this problem is to convert them into *index numbers,* choosing a suitable *base date* (in this case, April Year One) and calling the figures at that date 100. Between April and June of Year One other currency deposits rose by 7.6 per cent from £1,458 million to £1,569 million. With April Year One = 100, the index number for June is 107.6. Care is needed when comparing movements in the two indices. In the period under review sterling deposits rose by 28 per cent (the index number for April Year Two was 128) whilst there was a much bigger increase of 65 per cent for other currency deposits. However, the latter were still relatively unimportant, accounting for only about 10 per cent of total deposits at the end of the period compared with just over 8 per cent at the beginning.

Section D of Fig. 8 illustrates even more clearly the need for caution when interpreting charts and diagrams. The chart in this case has been designed to show how the deposit growth of various categories of bank compares with that of the Clearing Banks over a one-year period. The very favourable growth rate (55 per cent) of the

Northern Ireland banks is clearly much better than that for the Clearers (28 per cent), whilst the Merchant Banks or Accepting Houses did much worse (5 per cent). One danger is that people using the chart will overlook the fact that it deals only with part of the deposit picture: sterling deposits; there is no mention of deposits of other currencies. Because the purpose was to show changes for the period as a whole, monthly figures have been omitted. The danger here is that we are then unable to discern *trends* in the figures. Thus one group of banks may have obtained peak deposits earlier in the year and at the end of the period may be losing them rapidly whilst others may still be steadily rising. There is also a false impression that the trend for all groups is upwards, and there is the danger of being misled by a proportionate increase when actual figures are not known. Although the percentage increase of Northern Ireland bank deposits was very good, the actual rise was only £256m compared with a rise for the Clearing Banks of well over £4,000m. Despite their good performance, Northern Ireland bank deposits were still only about a thirtieth of Clearing Banks deposits at the end of the period.

EFFECTIVE COMMUNICATION

Communication by means of statistical charts and diagrams is only a minor part of the subject of communication. Ideas, feelings and emotions as well as information are among the things people communicate to one another. Writing and the spoken word are obviously very important but there are many other forms including the visual arts, the way people dress and their physical movements. What is communicated by someone wearing long hair and dirty jeans is quite different from that of someone dressed in a dark suit and white collar! The impression created by a manager thumping his desk is quite different from that conveyed when he gives you a friendly pat on the shoulder. Human communication is frequently very subtle – a raised eyebrow, a steely glance – and is one of the main features distinguishing man from other members of the animal kingdom.

There are, however, certain important principles which must be remembered by all concerned with management. Communication always involves at least two people. It involves mechanisms both for transmitting and receiving signals, and various barriers exist which obstruct the process. As can be seen from Fig. 9, good communication

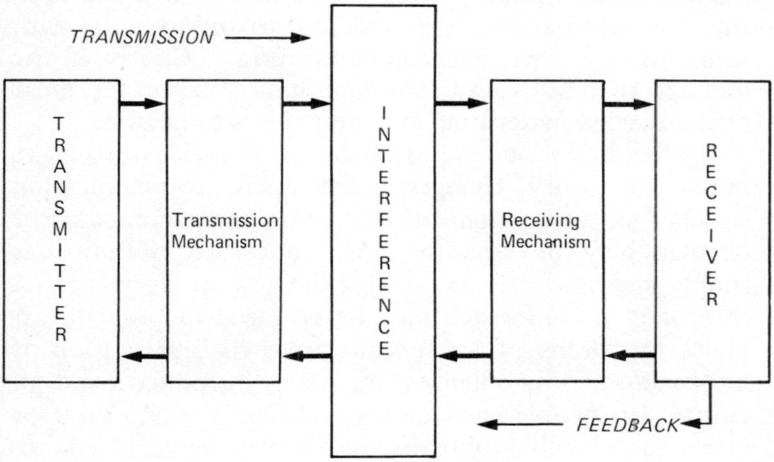

Fig. 9. A communication system.

involves a feedback mechanism to ensure that the process is functioning properly. Thus, when an instruction is given, it is important to know that it has been understood: it is not sufficient for the recipient to say he understands or for him just to think he does.

It follows from this that before good communication can take place, the transmitter must have a clear idea of what he wishes to transmit. It is no good issuing an instruction unless you know precisely what you want other people to do. "Think before you speak" is an adage well worth remembering. It applies to whatever is to be coummunicated, not only to information but also to the ideas and attitudes that one is attempting to put over.

If the views of other people are being sought, it is worth first asking yourself what it is you want to know! What facts do you require? About what precisely are you seeking opinions?

It is important also to consider the best transmission and receiving mechanisms to be used, whether, for example, it is better to have a word with someone over the 'phone or to ask them to see you: whether a letter or memorandum would be better: whether, after a conversation has taken place, it is desirable to follow it up with some form of written communication. Clearly if the message that has to be communicated is important, great care is needed in deciding how best this is to be done.

If a bank is about to introduce a new service or to make important policy changes, a complete communication strategy has to be planned. First of all a memorandum or circular may be sent to those concerned outlining as simply and as clearly as possible the new arrangements. A little later a conference may be arranged in order to explain, by means of a carefully prepared presentation of information, why changes are being introduced and to ensure that people have understood clearly what exactly is intended. Small group discussion may be arranged, together with question and answer sessions and in appropriate cases some form of test may be introduced to make sure that people have understood what is required of them.

For good communication to take place it is essential that receivers as well as transmitters realise that they have a part to play in the process. "What is the best way of getting the message across?" asks the transmitter, "What is he trying to say?" questions the receiver.

Both have to overcome interference, the barrier – analogous to the crackling on a telephone line – which prevents good communication. Its nature varies. Often ideas are expressed in an unnecessarily complex way, or too many words are used when a few would do. Messages should be kept as short and simple as possible, jargon should be avoided where its use is inappropriate, the quantity of material communicated should be kept to a minimum – people can get drowned in a sea of paper, they can get tired of listening to a long-winded explanation. The state of mind of the receiver, his lack of receptivity, is a very frequent barrier: a set pattern of thinking, a rigid set of attitudes often make it difficult to get a message across. The words may be understood, but lack of true comprehension inhibits response. Because of this, and when the message is important, multiple communication channels are used – a written document followed by spoken and visual presentation at a conference. Where a major change of attitude is sought, communication may have to take place over an extended period, message following message in a variety of ways, each reinforcing the last. Sometimes it proves impossible to achieve the required change and then it is that we hear such phrases as "golden handshake", "early retirement" and "sideways promotion".

DISCUSSION QUESTIONS

1. What methods of communication are used by staff working in your office?
2. How would your work be improved by having an increased and improved flow of information?
3. How could the improved flow of information mentioned in Question 2 be obtained, and at what cost?
4. Consider the ways in which you talk to people at work – other staff, customers, visitors and officials from Head Office or other branches and offices. Account for any differences in the style you use.
5. List some of the types of information you use during your day's work.
6. Why are good communication and information systems needed for the control of a bank system?

7. Outline a monitoring system to control your own work.
8. How is the information you use at work communicated to you?
9. What do you understand by variance analysis and why is it useful?
10. Explain the differences between profit, responsibility and cost centres.

CHAPTER V

Managing Human Resources

"... it is the intention to regulate the flow of new entrants year by year in accordance with a long-term plan, so that in due course the male staff will be more or less evenly distributed in ages from 17 up to 60 years."

Sir Charles Lidbury, formerly Chief General Manager, Westminister Bank Limited. November 1946.

HUMAN RESOURCES

Economists talk frequently about the factors of production needed to produce the goods and services we consume. In the final analysis these factors fall into two major classes, human and non-human resources. The standard of living enjoyed by the world's population depends on the ability of men and women to organise their affairs so as to obtain the maximum benefit from the Earth's resources. An individual country's living standards depend on its endowment of natural resources and the efforts of its people.

A bank, like other corporate bodies, is slightly different for it is an artifical creation with no natural boundaries. However, it is part of a national economic system and like that system depends on resources for its existence. These resources come together as inputs into the bank system. Thus a computer installation or the materials to build bank premises are the result of applying labour to natural resources.

Money, a crucial bank input, fits uneasily into our definition of resources for it has a nature of its own which can only be understood by studying monetary economic theory. The most important resource required by a bank is people. Being a human creation, it needs human beings to run it. There would be no buildings or equipment unless this input had been arranged by people, and no money input unless there were people around to receive it. Despite the development of computers and the introduction of other mechanical aids, banking is still a labour intensive industry. A bank's labour force can be regarded as its most important asset, each unit of which is unique and, being human, demands human treatment.

Dealing with staff is the most difficult aspect of management, both fascinating and rewarding but often the most frustrating. Despite all the problems of providing buildings and equipment or of dealing with technological change, there is nothing more difficult than building and maintaining a work force which is efficient, effective and well-motivated.

MOTIVATION

It was pointed out on pp. 10 and 11 that the way staff are treated depends on the management style of the bank as a whole and of individual managers. There is no unique prescription: each manager must discover and develop his own style, testing and adapting it in the field of experience. The only true way of judging his effectiveness is by the results he obtains within the limits imposed upon him. Whether he is aloof or friendly, bullying or persuasive matters little; it is the long-run results that matter.

A manager must be adaptable. The characteristics of the staff body change, the age structure alters, there are changes in the ratio of male to female staff. A manager may have to adapt from running a small office with an experienced staff to a larger office with younger people whose lack of experience is matched by youthful vigour. Political and socio-economic changes take place, unions become stronger and more militant; full employment encourages a less submissive attitude. The effect of better educational facilities may be to make people question more readily why a certain action is proposed. Management, like politics, is the *art of the possible*. The difficulty is knowing what is possible. This is particularly true when dealing with human beings for we can never know with certainty how a person will perform until he is put to the test. It would be a lucky person who could claim with sincerity that he had been happy throughout his working life whatever job he had had to do. It follows that aiming for a *happy* staff is idealistic: a better aim might be to have a *contented* staff, but this implies that people are content with their present lot and thus lack drive and ambition, an unhealthy situation. Much better to create conditions in which staff find their work *satisfying* both in an emotional and pecuniary sense. Fellow workers are rather like relations; we are forced to get on with them, we only choose our friends! But that need not prevent our work being satisfying, and the more satisfying it is the better motivation is likely to be. Work satisfaction comes from a number of sources: from the knowledge of a job well done, from the realisation that others recognise the fact, from the standard of living we and our families are able to enjoy, from status and power, and from the knowledge that promotion could enhance satisfaction from these sources – a better salary, improved status, more interesting work.

Behavioural scientists have done a good deal of work on motivation and job satisfaction and a knowledge of the literature can be rewarding. But groups of workers differ in their attitudes, and management needs to determine the forces motivating different groups, both within the bank as a whole and within individual offices. A manager may find that some of his staff are interested only in the money they earn and their working conditions. Others will be interested in promotion, in learning how to improve their current performance and how to tackle more demanding work. Good management tries to identify the forces motivating staff and strives to harness them to achieve the bank's objectives.

HUMAN RELATIONS

Our friend Smith tried to do this when he took up his first management post. During the first weeks at the branch he found time to talk to each member of the staff. Some of the girls seemed to be more interested in affairs of the heart than those of the bank, but he was able to put over his views on how a telephone should be answered and the importance of good personal appearance. He was disappointed that the security and foreign clerks showed little enthusiasm when he spoke of his plans for increasing branch business although they seemed pleased when he told them it was not his intention to supervise their work closely and that they need only refer to him if something unusual cropped up.

Two young men on the staff interested him, mainly because of the differences in their temperaments and abilities. Discussing their career prospects, he suggested to one who had already completed his banking diploma that some part-time teaching at the Polytechnic would help him consolidate his knowledge and would be quite profitable. The other, although intelligent, was still struggling with final examination subjects. He confessed that he found the work dull and uninteresting and that he found it difficult to become enthusiastic over banking technicalities. He was wondering whether to leave the bank and start a new career altogether. Smith talked about some of the new services the bank had introduced and about the interesting opportunities that existed. He advised him to complete his examinations as quickly as possible and to consider what other jobs in the bank appealed to him. He promised that when the examinations were out of the way he would arrange for him to visit one of the bank's computer centres so that he could see the work done there.

MANAGEMENT BY OBJECTIVES

Smith had made a few tentative steps towards *Manage-*

ment by Objectives (MBO). This approach to management is a *total* approach, one which extends the notion of corporate planning and control into the field of personnel management. As John Humble has said:

> "it is a dynamic system which seeks to integrate the company's need to clarify and achieve its profit and growth goals with the manager's need to contribute and develop himself. It is a demanding and rewarding style of managing a business."

The extent to which MBO will be developed within a particular bank must obviously vary. If fully implemented, the corporate planning process – deciding policy and developing a corporate strategy – will be developed, through tactical planning, into detailed plans, targets and objectives for individual managers. Managers will be expected to involve their staff in the planning process, different sections of an office or branch being made aware of what is expected of them as a contribution to the overall objectives of the business.

Smith failed to do this. He outlined plans for branch development but established no individual staff objectives. Most people when told by the manager that he wants to open fifty accounts in ten months are likely to show only polite interest and to say to themselves "So what?" MBO seeks to counter this by encouraging managers to discuss with subordinates what part they can play. Their progress is monitored and advice is given to help them meet the objectives, where necessary additional training being arranged. In an ideal situation, their success is measured against the goals that have been set and is recognised within the salary structure or by changes in promotion prospects.

HUMAN DEVELOPMENT

MBO is important because of its concern with individual

development, Smith's interest in the careers of the two young male members of staff exemplifying this approach. Managers as well as their staff are encouraged to recognise their weaknesses and to do something about them, seeking ways in which they may be overcome. Regional managers, for example, will discuss with each manager in the region what he can contribute to its progress and what should be his targets for the year. Clearly-defined targets are then agreed, the aim being to set them at a level which stimulates effort and engenders satisfaction when they are met. Obviously targets which are set too high and which are beyond the bounds of possibility are of no use, either to the bank or to individuals. A manager is able to assess his progress and at the year-end he is judged by his results, care being taken to allow for unusual circumstances, such as the unavoidable loss of an important account.

JOB ENRICHMENT

Increasingly, modern management seeks to take account of the human factor, of the need to motivate people and to make their job more satisfying. More attention is now paid to *job enrichment* as a reaction to the standardisation and specialisation found in industry, where the typical assembly line associated with mass production methods can lead to boredom, fatigue, frustration and low morale. These in turn lower the quality of work, lead to more absences and grievances and encourage a feeling of hostility towards management.

When applied to industry, job enrichment is likely to consist of the re-arrangement of production facilities in groups of machines or equipment which are operated by a team of workers jointly responsible for some identifiable product such as a car or bicycle. Each worker has to undertake a variety of tasks and much repetitive work is eliminated. The alleviation of job monotony and the satisfaction of helping to produce a recognisable product increases job satisfaction and motivation. Efficiency, it is claimed, improves and this in turn improves job satisfaction through the knowledge that a job has been well done.

A useful example of job enrichment in banking can be drawn from the work of cashiers. It illustrates also the difficulty of deciding about one's attitude. The basic tasks of a bank cashier are the receipt of credits and the payment of cash. But the role may be more broadly defined, the cashier being required to undertake other tasks such as dealing with cheque books, bank statements, bankers' orders and perhaps even with travel business. Where branch size makes it possible, there are advantages in defining the cashier's role as narrowly as possible. From the point of view of a customer wishing to pay in a credit, or cash a cheque, there may be a prolonged wait if the cashier has to deal with a variety of services for other customers. From the bank's point of view there are also gains: cashier training programmes can be shorter thus saving money, particularly where staff turnover is high; it may be possible to use a lower calibre of staff thus making recruitment easier and possibly reducing the level of salaries that have to be paid; by simplifying the tasks to be performed the adoption of mechanical aids is made easier, with possibly a reduction in cost levels.

All this, however, goes against the spirit of job enrichment, which argues that jobs should be made more interesting and meaningful. By simplifying the cashier's work it could be that motivation is diminished and staff turnover increased. There may be a reduction in the willingness of cashiers to identify with the work of the branch as a whole; customers may cease to be regarded as human beings and the orientation may be towards passing items backwards and forwards over the counter rather than providing a service for the person on the other side. For these reasons the job may become less attractive, with a consequent fall in the calibre of people interested in carrying it out.

JOB ANALYSIS

In due course it may well be that the work of a cashier will become quite different from what it is now. By reducing the range of tasks to be undertaken it may be that mechanical aids can be developed which take over completely what are now regarded as the basic functions. The development of cash dispensers, change-giving machines and other equipment may free cashiers – if that remains their best description – for other tasks such as dealing with enquiries and giving advice on the use of bank services. Job enrichment may in the end be best obtained by first simplifying the job and making it less interesting!

The strategy to be adopted with cashiers is clearly a management decision which has to take account of many factors such as the availability of new staff and technological developments within the equipment field. Clearly, too, management needs to consider the role of other groups of staff, to analyse jobs generally and to establish *job descriptions* or *job specifications*. The precise nature of these will depend on the attitude of management and on its willingness to devote resources to the task. At branch or departmental level it can be interesting and very salutary to attempt to define the job of each member of staff; the tasks to be performed, the people to whom he is responsible for the effective performance of these tasks and the people who are responsible to him for the performance of their tasks. The limits on each staff member's freedom of action can be set down, as well as the names of those with authority to give him a decision when this has to be sought. When the precise nature of a job has been defined, it is possible to consider the qualities and aptitudes needed for its succesful performance; for example, the level of educational attainment and training needed and the amount of prior knowledge and experience that is required. When *staff appraisal* is being undertaken – possibly through the preparation of an annual report – it is possible to measure performance against established targets and the qualities and aptitudes of the member of staff concerned with those set out in the job description. It may, for example, be found that poor performance can be accounted for by lack of training in a particular skill and that if this is remedied both bank and employee will benefit. It may be discovered that the job requires certain qualities not possessed by the person holding the post, that he is unable, for example, to cope with large quantities of routine boring work, but that he has accounting skills above the average. Clearly, in this case, it would be to everybody's advantage if there could be a move to a job where these skills could be fully used.

JOB DESCRIPTIONS

To assist its planning and control systems, a bank, particularly if it has a large staff, may decide to establish job descriptions or specifications for the major categories of work. These could be established in broad terms possibly under the headings shown in the example for a credit officer in Fig. 10. Standards are thereby established which can be helpful to those occupying or about to occupy a new post as well as to those responsible for staff performance and potential. Proper integration within the corporate planning process is also assisted. Thus, if there are plans to increase the extent of medium-term lending it may have important implications for the work of credit officers and these can be considered carefully and the job specification amended accordingly.

Staff recruitment, selection, training, development and promotion must all be consonant with the needs of the bank, and up-to-date job descriptions help to ensure that this is so They can be helpful too in *salary administration* where jobs are grouped into specific grades, comparisons being made with similar work by staff in other organisations. The aim should be to provide a salary structure geared both to the present and future needs of the bank. Where job descriptions are drawn up in greater detail to cover individual posts in a branch or department, this can

CREDIT OFFICER

I *Duties:*
Advances Approvals
Monitoring Advances
Security Control

II *Authority:*
Discretionary Limits
Terms for Advance
Interest Rates

III *Educational Requirements:*
Sound knowledge of — Banking Law and Practice
— Accounting Statements and Ratios
— Current Economic and Financial Conditions

IV *Training Requirements:*
Attend Bank Courses — Security Clerks' Course
Junior Management Course

V *Experience:*
Branch/Departmental
Domestic/International

VI *Aptitudes:*
Sound Judgment
Good Human Relations
Good Communication — Written
Oral

VII *Technical:*
Up-to-date knowledge of Standing Instructions
Procedures Manual
Head Office Circulars

Fig. 10. Outline job description.

help the difficult task of *delegation* by making it clear which responsibilities have been delegated and who is responsible for ensuring that they are properly exercised.

DISCUSSION QUESTIONS

1. A customer writes to complain that a member of your staff has been rude to him over the telephone.

Outline the action you would take.

2. What is your bank's policy on the way staff should dress? Whose responsibility is it to inform new staff of this policy?

3. You receive an anonymous letter accusing one of your staff of immoral behaviour. What would you do?

4. A hard-working, intelligent member of your staff continues to arrive late for work despite frequent warnings. He would be difficult to replace but other staff are complaining. What would you do?

5. You are required to estimate the staffing requirements of your office on an annual basis for the next five years as well as suggesting a provisional figure for ten years ahead. How would you set about this task and what information would you need?

6. Prepare detailed job descriptions for two members of your staff.

7. A young South African member of your staff sees you to discuss his career prospects. He has a second class degree (lower division) from the London School of Economics and says he is interested in the economic development of Brazil. He is very interested in banking but would rather study for a research degree than take the examinations of the Institute of Bankers. What advice would you give him?

8. You receive a confidential letter from a customer saying she thinks she received one pound short in cash recently. The cashier concerned has a bad record of till shortages. What, if anything, would you say to the cashier?

9. A trade union official writes asking if he can come and talk to the staff of your office at a convenient time. You are a member of a different union. What would you do?

10. You have been asked to help a staff recruiting drive by opening your branch to sixth formers interested in banking as a career. What arrangements would you make?

CHAPTER VI

Bank Marketing

"There are few things that try a man's temper more than to be kept waiting a long time at a banker's counter."

J. W. Gilbart

THE MARKETING APPROACH

A bank which believes that its main task is to discover its customers' needs and then sets out to satisfy them can be said to be "marketing-orientated". This orientation applies to existing and new services, both of which should be covered by a bank's *marketing strategy*, which is an important ingredient of the total strategy arrived at during the corporate planning process.

It is likely that the main corporate objective will be to raise profits by an agreed percentage over the planning period. It is possible that if the bank continues on its existing operational path with no remedial action, profits will decline. This profit path over an assumed five-year planning period is illustrated in Fig. 11, which shows that if the profit target is to be attained this downward drift of profits must be halted and the trend reversed. In considering its strategy the bank has to consider what, if any, new services can be profitably introduced. In our example, the bank has adopted a two-fold strategy, the plan being to make existing services profitable and thus halt the downward drift and at the same time to introduce new services which, when they come "on stream" in two

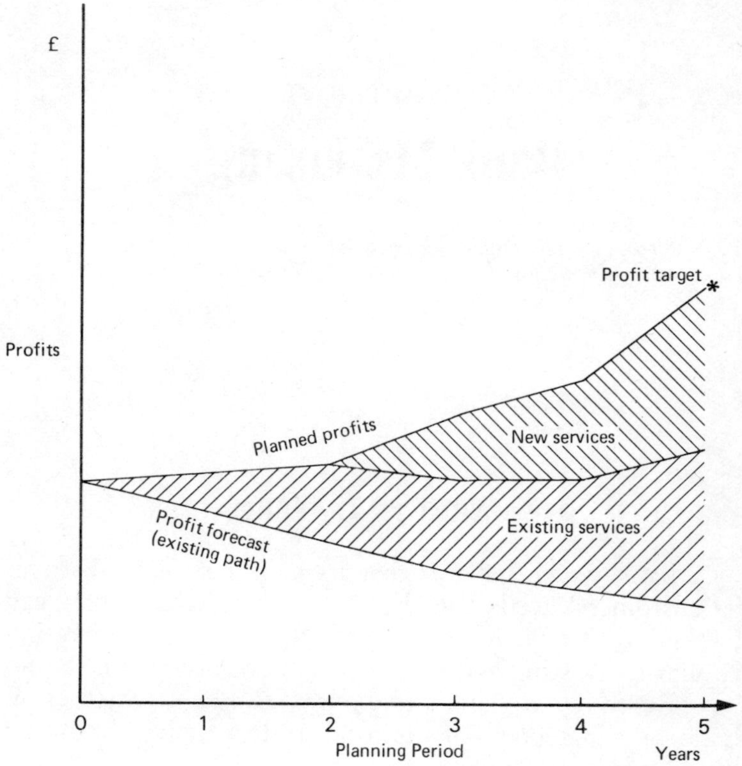

Fig. 11. **Profit planning.**

or three years, will generate higher profits and allow the five-year profit target to be reached.

PRODUCTION ORIENTATION

It is quite possible for a bank or any other firm to survive for many years by providing a well-established range of goods or services for which there appears to be a steady and continuing market. Management is efficient in the sense that it concentrates on providing a sound product, on ensuring that the business runs effectively, that costs are kept down and that modern methods of operation are introduced. The orientation of a bank run in this way is towards the input and "black box" part of the system rather than to the output side, to the left-hand side of Fig. 5 rather than to the right.

Now clearly it is highly desirable that a bank's management should concern itself closely with the efficiency of day-to-day operations, with staff recruitment, the provision of adequate accommodation and other facilities, but the orientation is wrong for it is directed away from the output side of the system. Banks operate in a dynamic environment and they must adjust their output to meet changing needs. Failure to move quickly enough means that the public's needs will always be ahead of the service provided: a bank will find that other institutions are providing services it could provide or that its share of total advances or deposits is falling.

A marketing orientation implies that management's first task is to decide what services to provide, and in what form. The decisions taken will determine the type and amount of inputs needed by the system and how they should be used to generate the desired output. In some cases, restraints may be imposed by the lack of suitable inputs or by technical difficulties in organising them. A bank system must therefore be seen in its totality, with the emphasis on the output side. The present and future demand for each existing and prospective new service has to be considered and an appropriate strategy formulated.

The concept of a *product life cycle* illustrated in Fig. 12, particularly applicable where consumer goods are concerned, provides a useful way of looking at bank services. When a service is introduced for the first time there is likely to be a period during which demand grows slowly as the public becomes aware of its existence and value. Profits may accrue only towards the end of this period but may then be expected to increase as the service comes to be accepted and the demand for it grows. With the passage of time demand is likely to level off as saturation point is reached and as competitors start offering the

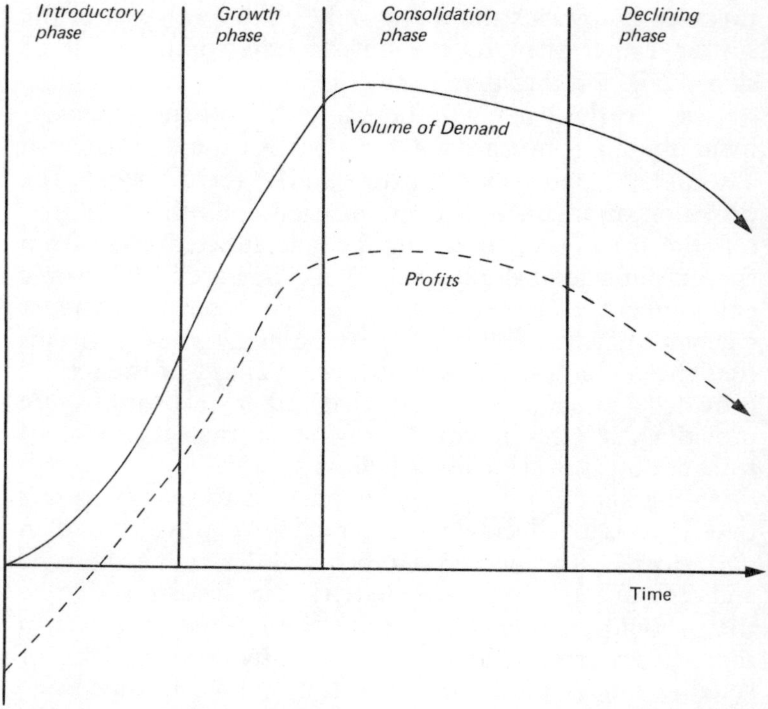

Fig. 12. Product life cycle for a bank service.

same service. In the final phase, a reduction in demand and thus of profits may occur as other banks step up their competition and introduce improved features to their competing service. It is easy to envisage this sequence of events with services such as credit cards, but less easy to recognise with established services such as bank lending. To some extent this is due to the long time-span involved, for it is evident that demand patterns do change, the decline of bill finance and the growth of the overdraft system in the nineteenth century providing one good example.

MARKETING MIX

The object of *market research* is to study these demand

patterns so as to determine as precisely as possible what the customer wants. Chapter IV showed that for successful planning and operating a bank needs to have a flow of information from both within and outside the organisation. An important part of this information is concerned with the pattern and nature of demand for the bank's output without which it is impossible to determine what should be the bank's marketing mix, that is, the number and type of services it should be offering. Increasingly, large banking groups are offering a wide variety of services, from insurance to leasing, and from consumer credit services to those concerned with corporate finance. It is a major responsibility of management to decide how many services are to be provided – bearing in mind that too great a variety could lead to inefficient operations – and how they are to be developed.

In seeking to discover what customers want from existing services and how good the prospects are for new services, a bank may draw on many sources of information. Its own internal records, effectively used, will indicate trends in the demand for the various services it offers although they will not reveal market potential or give an indication of latent needs. A good deal of this type of information may, however, be gleaned by the bank's staff particularly by those in close contact with customers and it is sound policy to encourage staff to collect this information and to provide formal or informal channels through which it can be collated and made available to those responsible for corporate planning.

In deciding on its marketing mix, a bank should make full use of all sources of published information. Estimates of the future level of income and how it will be distributed between different sections of the community, expected changes in the sex and age structure of the population and alterations in future employment patterns are among the things that will help determine what groups of customers the bank will need to serve when developing existing or future services. Information about the range of services offered in other countries and reports on the operations of other financial institutions are all helpful when developing a marketing strategy.

SEEKING ATTITUDES

But the only reliable way of finding out what people want, what they think about existing services or how they will react to new ones is to ask them. *Attitude surveys*, for example, may be conducted by means of questionnaires and interviews either by bank staff or by an outside agency, questions being asked to assess the efficiency, value and cost of the service provided. *Sample surveys* covering a cross-section of the population may be conducted to try to determine what use would be made of a new service if it were introduced. The use of informal surveys should not be overlooked. It is surprising the amount of information that can be gathered by a determined investigator during a short visit to a town where, by chatting to people in bus queues, shopkeepers and publicans it is possible, for example, to obtain a very clear picture of people's shopping patterns and the factors that determine them.

PRODUCT MARKETING

Having established a marketing strategy, determined the marketing mix and considered whether some product rationalisation is needed, a bank may set about introducing a new service. Any new product, be it a good or service, carries with it an element of risk and everything must be done to minimise this risk and to ensure that when the product is launched it proves a success. The bank has to be quite clear what the service is for and who is intended to use it. Only then can a closely defined *product strategy* be laid down.

New banking services introduced over recent years have included credit cards, certificates of deposit and special services for students and clearly there will be big differences in the strategy adopted for each product. But a number of questions common to all services must be answered. Where is the new product to be provided? Should credit cards be available throughout the country or confined to England and Wales? Why not Scotland? What about Northern Ireland? Are certificates of deposit to be issued only by Head Office? What about other major City offices and the large country branches? Are special student services to be available only in University towns or where there are Polytechnics? What about the students in Technical Colleges and Colleges of Education?

Another important range of questions comes under the heading of *sales promotion*. Is the new service to be brought to the attention of customers only, or non-customers, or both? Are there to be advertisements in magazines, the daily or weekly press, popular newspapers or the financial and quality press and banking and financial journals? What about radio and TV, posters on public hoardings, promotional literature in the bank's branches and offices? Is there to be a *sales campaign* and what form will it take? Will salesmen call on people's homes or will literature be sent through the post? Will telephone advertising be used? Decisions will have to be taken about the size of the advertising budget and how it can best be utilised, how long the advertising campaign is to last – a short series of full-page advertisements or a longer series of smaller ones – in other words whether there is to be an intensive or extensive campaign.

Difficult problems of *packaging* normally do not arise where services are concerned: unlike goods there are no transport difficulties or bulk breaking and storage problems. On the other hand the "silent salesman" aspect of marketing needs careful consideration. Thus in designing a credit card the aim must be to ensure that not only is it functionally perfect (can it be signed easily?) but also that its appearance is attractive to the user. Likewise the envelopes used by the credit card service must have customer appeal and must be designed with the schedule of production costs as well as functional and aesthetic requirements in mind.

Product pricing has to be considered at an early stage, for until it is known what charge, if any, is to be made for the service it is not possible to make sound decisions about the costs that may be incurred by those responsible for introducing it. Where possible, forecasts have to be made of the volume of demand likely to arise at different prices so that income estimates can be prepared. With information about future costs and income it is possible to forecast when the new service will "break even" for, as shown in Fig. 12, losses are likely to arise at least in the early stages of the introductory phase and these have to be provided for. *Product testing* and *test marketing* also have to be considered so as to ensure success after the service has been launched. Whilst it is not usually possible to test a bank service by introducing it in a small geographical area, it may be possible with some services to make them available to a limited number of customers to see how they respond. In other cases, it may be possible to limit the service to bank staff so that a trial run can be conducted to check that unforseeen difficulties do not arise when operations commence. In short, the essential task is to use imagination and foresight to ensure that everything is done to ensure the profitability of the new service.

BRANCH MARKETING

The idea that a bank should be marketing-orientated applies equally to its constituent parts, whether operating at local or regional level at home or overseas. The question must be asked "Who are our customers and prospective customers, what are their needs and which of the bank's services can we sell profitably to them?"

To answer these questions a branch manager needs an intimate knowledge of his area so that he may evaluate the changes taking place and decide what opportunities there are for profitable development. He should know what changes are taking place in the size and composition of the local population, in the pattern of local employment and in people's shopping habits. Even in an apparently stable situation he should assume that changes are occurring and should seek to discover what they are. The relocation of a school may affect shopping habits and suggest the need for a new sub-branch, the redevelopment of old residential property may point to coming changes in population density levels and an increase in demand for bank services. Ethnic changes, commercial and industrial development schemes, changes in leisure pursuits, all need to be recognised and their effect on business considered. For one manager it may be important to be abreast of developments taking place in agriculture, for another changes in industrial processes may be significant.

PUBLIC RELATIONS

The local manager has an important *public relations* job to carry out. The bank has to project a corporate image acceptable to the population as a whole. If it is a large bank it will be serving almost every section of the community and it needs to show that it is an organisation operating efficiently, with integrity and with a proper regard to its public responsibilities. Good relations with the national press and other branches of the media must be established and an acceptable flow of information about the bank's activities must be generated. The attitude of different sections of the reading public must be recognised; for example, readers of the financial and the popular press will have different views on what is an acceptable level of bank profits. In a similar way, the local manager must be sensitive to the differing views of people he meets within the narrower community his branch serves.

Those operating at the point of sale, the branches which are in continuous contact with the public, have an especially important public relations role to play, possibly the most important of all. The main contact with customers is over the bank counter, by telephone and in the manager's room. But there are other important contacts, the manager with the local press and with industry and commerce, and the branch staff as a whole through its social contact within the local community. It is important that staff realise this and that the bank's recruitment, promotion and training policies are all geared to this situation.

The key man in the bank's hierarchy is the branch manager who has been described as the "G.P. of the financial world" and one of the banks' big staff headaches.

> "Look at his job. He has long had to run an office efficiently, to advise on personal financial problems, to judge credit risks and to sort out companies' balance sheets. Now he is expected to act as salesman for the bank too. Yet he has virtually no training – bar experience – for the job."*

Clearly, changes in staffing policies will in time help to cure the headache, but a good deal can be achieved through the planning processes, by introducing, for example, an MBO approach, by re-thinking job descriptions and by defining objectives and establishing targets which the bank then helps its mangers to achieve. When this is done it should no longer be possible to describe the branch manager's job as *"virtually impossible".* *

DISCUSSION QUESTIONS

1. Consider a bank service which is in the declining phase and suggest what action the bank should take.
2. What do you understand by the phrase "marketing mix" and what is its relevance to banking?

*Hamish McRae and Frances Cairncross: *Capital City, London as a Financial Centre* (Eyre Methuen, 1973).

3. What information would you seek when developing a market strategy for the branch of a bank?
4. What is meant when a bank is said to be "marketing-orientated"?
5. "Test marketing cannot be applied in banking." Do you consider this is true?
6. What factors have to be taken into account when deciding what to charge for a bank service?
7. "A complete change in training programmes will be needed as banks become more competitive." How far do you think this is true, and why?
8. "The difficulty of marketing bank services is that they all look the same whichever bank provides them." Discuss.
9. Do you think that branch managers should be required actively to solicit business within the community?
10. A reporter from the local newspaper telephones to say he is calling to see you next week in connection with a series of "profiles" he is preparing for his paper. What would you do?

CHAPTER VII

The Tools of Management

"...place the desk of the chief or head clerk in such a position that he can see all over the office. 'A master's eye will do more work than both his hands.' "

J. W. Gilbart

DEVELOPING A MANAGEMENT ATTITUDE

Marketing, as we have seen, is not merely a collection of techniques but rather – and more importantly – an attitude of mind. If a bank is marketing-orientated the need to employ marketing techniques emerges naturally as management starts to consider the services it should provide and how sales of these services can best be promoted.

Modern management represents a positive approach to the task of running an institution successfully, to planning, organising, directing, co-ordinating and controlling human and other resources so as to achieve, as efficiently and as effectively as possible, a range of stated objectives. Management is an art because it is a human activity, in which human beings have to make decisions and in which human beings have to organise the activities of other human beings. If not a science, modern management has become more scientific, with scientific method being applied increasingly to management processes. This implies getting at the facts, making decisions, translating these decisions into action and monitoring the results.

Ideas drawn from many branches of human knowledge are encompassed by "management". Economics, for example, points to the importance of using scarce resources to maximise returns whilst accounting provides the techniques for measuring progress, assisting decision-making and exercising control. Sociology and psychology, disciplines concerned with human behaviour, clearly have a part to play in management, a part which may well become more important, helping us to understand with greater clarity why, for instance, some staff work with enthusiasm whilst others seem bored and badly motivated. A manager must be aware of these ideas and must also have sufficient knowledge of the techniques available, some of them highly sophisticated, to enable him to judge when to call upon the services of an expert.

ORGANISATION

A good deal of early work in management was concerned with the study of organisations to discover how time and effort could be used to best advantage. Very often large firms established an *Organisation and Methods* team whose job was to provide advice on the structure of the firm, its management and control and its systems, procedures and methods. Formal structures, patterns of responsibility and their inter-relationships are often illustrated by an *organisation chart* showing, in diagrammatic form, lines of authority and the distribution of functions. Figure 13 shows graphically how the role of a deputy manager can differ quite radically depending on how he is seen as fitting into the management structure.

MANAGEMENT TECHNIQUES

Work Study is a generic term covering techniques used in examining human work in all its aspects, which has been developed in order to improve efficiency and increase profitability. It usually embraces method study and work measurement also. A closely allied activity is *Office Planning*, which concerns itself with office layout, seeking to locate staff in the most effective way. Lighting, noise levels, decor – including the best colour scheme – heating

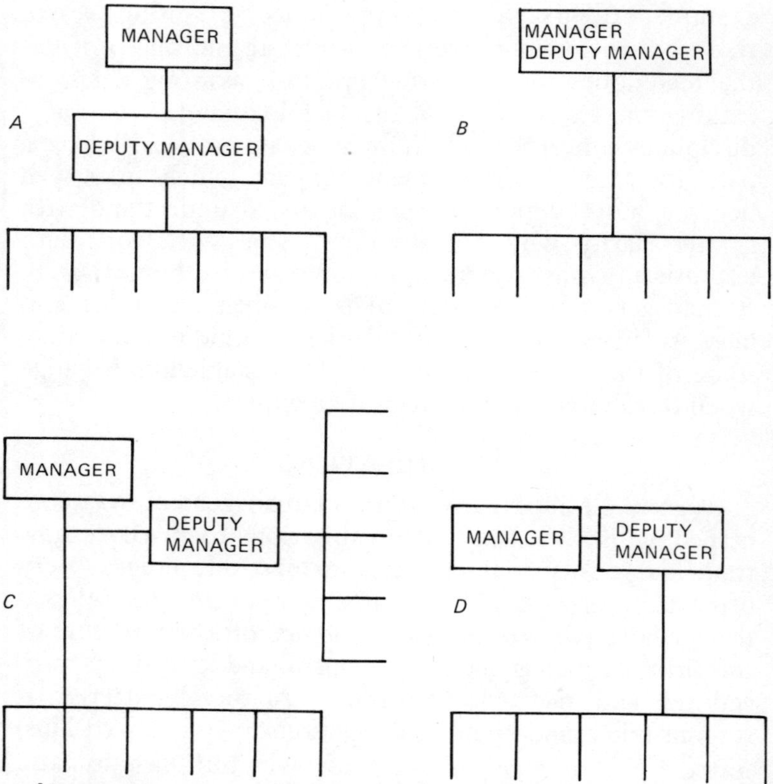

[Courtesy D. A. Brown, The Technical Journal, Vol. 12 No. 7, New Series.]

Fig. 13. Organisation charts: the role of the deputy manager.

and humidity are now well recognised as factors with a significant effect on the level of office efficiency.

Method Study deals with the way in which a particular task is carried out. Critical examination often leads to greater efficiency: redesign of forms can lead to a saving of paper and speedier processing: improved filing systems can save time and money. *Work Measurement* is often used when determining staff establishment levels. It enables staff to be allocated so that the work load is shared between them in an equitable way. Where the job is of a routine nature, work measurement is not too difficult, but problems arise where the flow of work is irregular or where "case work" is involved. The time and effort devoted to different cases by a credit officer dealing with advances can vary enormously and it has sometimes been suggested that the easiest means of measurement would be by weighing the amount of paper dealt with – probably not a very useful or acceptable procedure! Another closely-related technique is *Time Study*, which is really part of work measurement. This seeks to establish norms for particular tasks which enable management to monitor the efficiency and effectiveness of the individual worker.

Human performance is the subject matter of *Ergonomics*, the study of relationships between workers and their environment, and in particular the application of anatomical, physiological and psychological knowledge. The worker and his job are studied as a whole and equipment is designed accordingly. The aim is to reduce stress, loss of efficiency through fatigue and to assess the exact amount of energy needed to perform a particular task. In banking, Ergonomics might be applied to the design of desks and seating, to the positioning of office equipment, to the arrangement of controls on a calculating machine, or to the design of hardware for a computer installation.

Quality Control has just as much application in a bank as it does in a factory manufacturing nuts and bolts. Decisions have to be made about the standard of quality to be achieved, bearing in mind that the quality of a service is closely related to the time and effort spent in producing it. For example, letters, reports and memoranda can be improved and re-written, but this increases costs. Likewise the standard of service to customers can be improved but often only by increasing costs. A bank has to decide on the standard to be adopted – passbooks, handwritten with a quill pen, or computerised statements – and clearly its decision will reflect the needs it has perceived in its customers. Having determined the standard for each service a system is needed to ensure that it is maintained. Excessive checking increases costs, often out of proportion to the results achieved; too little checking leads to an unacceptable level of customer complaint or to banking losses. Checking can be on a random or 100 per cent basis or statistical methods and sampling techniques can be adopted to ensure that the standard of work remains within prescribed limits. *Cybernetic Control* systems can be introduced which allow automatic remedial action to be taken when these limits are exceeded.

PLANNING CHARTS

In order to clarify thinking when a complex operation is being undertaken it is often helpful to use a chart to show

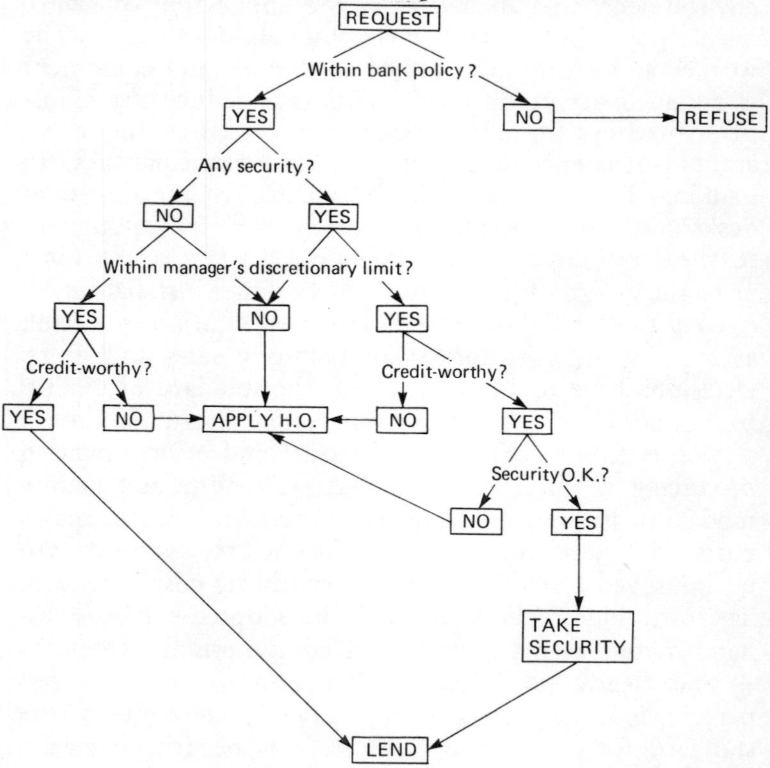

Fig. 14. Flow chart: bank lending.

the constituent events in their logical order. In Fig. 14 a *Flow Chart* has been used to show what might happen when a branch manager has to consider a request for an advance. Not all bankers would agree with the chart's logic – should a request which falls outside bank policy ever be refused outright? Should credit-worthiness be considered at an earlier stage in the sequence of events? Nevertheless, the chart probably illustrates fairly closely what takes place in the real banking world.

It will be seen that, apart from refusing a request, there are six possible outcomes from the branch manager's point of view. He can make an advance provided he is happy about the borrower's credit-worthiness and the sum involved falls within his discretionary limit. He can make an unsecured advance or, provided the security is in order, a secured one. There are four circumstances when the request has to be referred to Head Office:

1. When it falls outside the manager's discretionary limit.
2. When it is within the discretionary limit but he does not consider the borrower credit-worthy: either (*a*) when security is offered, or (*b*) when there is no security.
3. When he is able and willing to grant a secured advance, but the security seems to be unsatisfactory.

The more complex an operation the more likely it is that the use of flow charts will help clarify thinking. In our over-simplified example, designed to illustrate a principle, no attempt has been made to deal with different types of bank lending, with repayment arrangements or with the rate of interest to be charged. Likewise the sequence of events that follows a decision – "take security", for example – has been ignored. It will be seen that flow charts can be useful when standardising procedures for routine operations. They are helpful in determining policy and can be valuable in the staff training process. They can also be very helpful when considering the series of events that will have to be carried out in a non-recurrent operation.

Decisions theory provides a somewhat similar technique, the *Decision Tree*, used in order to show the sequence of decisions that have to be taken and the outcome involved in each when a complex problem is being considered. Thus, when a bank is considering whether or not to introduce a new service, the first decision is whether to abandon the idea or to go ahead with it. If it decides to go ahead, it has to consider whether or not there should be a test marketing operation, and if this is carried out it then has to decide whether to abandon the project or to go ahead and offer the service to the public. At each decision point the cost and likely income from each possible decision has to be assessed and it is often helpful to evaluate also the probability of a certain result taking place.

If we feel that there is a 75 per cent chance of rain tomorrow, we say that the probability that it will rain is 0.75 and the probability that it will not rain is 0.25, the probabilities adding up always to 1.00. Expected results can be weighted by the estimated probabilities. Thus a decision to market the new service could lead to low, medium or high demand and to respective net pay-offs of −£200,000, +£200,000 +£1,000,000. If these possible outcomes have probabilities of 0.20, 0.50 and 0.30 respectively and the probabilities are used to weight the net pay-offs, we can calculate an expected value of +£360,000 as follows:

$$0.20 \times (-200{,}000) + 0.50 \times 200{,}000 + 0.30 \times 1{,}000{,}000 = +\ 360{,}000$$

This expected value can then be compared with the cost of abandoning the project and the appropriate decision taken.

CRITICAL PATH ANALYSIS

As well as the problems of deciding what to do, there are problems of how to do it and a number of associated techniques have been developed to assist the detailed planning of complicated projects. *Network Analysis*, *PERT* (programme evaluation and review technique) and *Critical Path Analysis* can be applied to a variety of projects, to the establishment of a new branch or department, the making of changes in existing work or moving staff to new locations. In Fig. 15 a simple network has been used to show how the main aspects of a new credit card service can be planned.

It is supposed that there are twelve main activities to be accomplished before the service can be launched, the most likely time for each to be completed being as follows:

Activity	Events	Most likely time (weeks)
Design system	(0,1)	26
Recruit key staff	(1,3)	6
Advance publicity	(0,2)	3
Train key staff	(3,7)	4
Install computer system	(1,4)	30
Design stationery	(1,5)	6
Sign up retailers	(2,9)	50
Stationery print: initial	(5,6)	5
Test run	(4,8)	4
Recruit and train operational staff	(7,10)	8
Material to retailers	(9,10)	8
Stationery print: final	(6,10)	8

On the diagram, activities are denoted by arrows and events by squares. A number of the activities can take place concurrently whilst others depend on the prior completion of another activity; thus it is not possible to commence the initial stationery print (5,6) before the

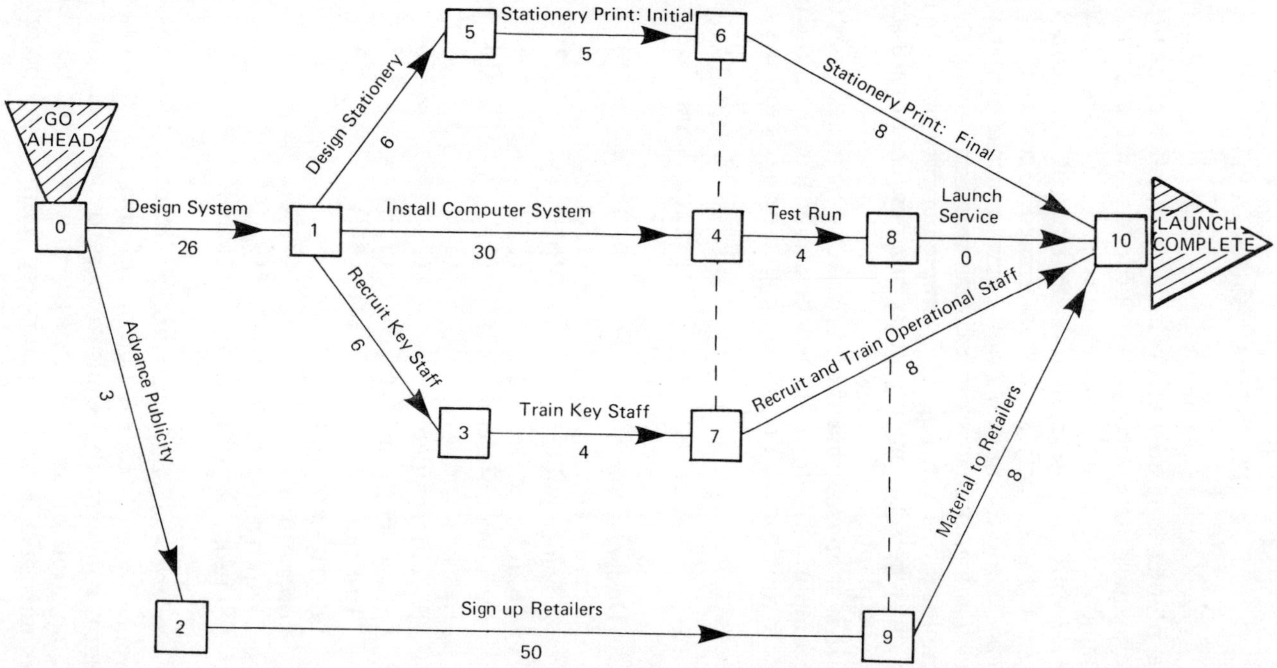

Fig. 15. **Critical path analysis: a credit card launch.**

stationery has been designed (1,5) and the only activity that can take place before the system is designed (0,1) is some advance publicity (0,2). The use of a dotted line represents a dummy activity and is inserted to ensure correct sequencing. The estimated time for each activity is indicated against the appropriate arrow.

An examination of the network shows that the new credit card service cannot be launched until sixty-eight weeks after the go-ahead has been given. Some activities must be completed before others commence, so that there is a critical path of events through the network. In this case, the critical path is given by events (0,1), (1,4), (4,8), and (9,10). Clearly there will be a reduction of time for the project if these events can be accomplished more quickly. Time can also be saved if the system is redesigned so that installation of the computer system, for example, can be started before the system design has been completed, if the time taken in sending material to retailers can be reduced or if it proves possible to commence this operation before the test run is completed.

The network also shows the best time for starting an activity or sequence of activities. Thus, if the stationery is designed and the initial print made immediately after the design of the system, stocks would have to be held for some time before they were required for the test run, resulting in the unnecessary tying up of capital. Likewise, it would be pointless to start the recruitment and training of key staff until about five weeks after the design of the system had been completed, for there would be no work for them to do.

Networks of this type are invaluable for those monitoring the progress of a project. Progress for each activity can be shown on a *Gantt Chart* which is used to measure work actually completed against what has been planned for an activity. Special attention has to be paid to those activities lying on the critical path and adjustments to plans have to be made when delays occur or when an activity is completed ahead of schedule.

DECISION-TAKING

The only certain thing about banking is that decisions have to be taken under conditions of uncertainty, and a variety of tools have been fashioned to assist managers with this difficult task. Readers who have covered the Accountancy syllabus of the Institute of Bankers will be familiar with the notions of *Net Present Value* and *Pay-back Period* and how these and *Discounted Cash Flow* (DCF) techniques can be used in the appraisal of capital projects. A rate of interest is applied to forecasts of additional outlay and income relating to a project so as to discount the future, discounting being necessary to take account of the fact that, even ignoring inflation, a pound today is worth more than a pound in a year's time because of the interest it could earn. Likewise, spending a pound now costs more than spending it in the future because of the interest that is foregone. Because of this, DCF techniques are particularly useful in comparing outcomes of alternative courses of action.

Operational Research, the application of scientific processes to operational problems, is being used increasingly in banking. *Linear Programming* is used to solve allocation problems – assigning limited resources to a number of activities in order to maximise returns. It can be used to help determine the allocation of staff, money, space and equipment for operations that can be performed in a variety of ways. Handling movements of bullion or planning the use of a bank's fleet of vehicles are possible applications. More important is the use of linear programming techniques in the management of bank assets, a very good example of an allocation problem.

Queueing Theory can be used to examine problems in which waiting periods are involved, for example, the extent to which waiting time will be increased if the arrival rate of customers at a bank counter goes up and how this waiting time can be restored to its original level. The techniques can be be used whenever units forming a queue arrive at random, whether these units are customers at the counter, applications for advances at Head Office or documentary credits in overseas branch.

Mathematical Models are increasingly being used – often with the assistance of a computer – to help solve difficult problems or forecast future events or simulate certain bank activites. These models are constructed from equations which show the relationship between different elements, some aspects of which can be controlled by management, and some not. An over-simplified example may help to explain how such models can be used in a bank.

Suppose a bank wishing to determine future profitability seeks as a first step to discover what changes are likely to take place in the level of all bank current account balances. Let us agree that these balances, D, are determined by real income, Y – the actual quantity of goods and services people can buy, the level of prices, P and the rate of interest, r. We say that the dependent variable D is determined by the independent variables. This can be shown as follows:

$$D = f(Y,P,r)$$

This is a shorthand which helps us very little, for it seems fairly obvious that if people's real income rises or prices go up they will need to keep more money on current account. Likewise, an increase in interest rates may be expected to encourage people to move money from current accounts into more rewarding fields. What we need is something more specific about the way in which the variables are related. Consider the following equation:

$$D = a + bY + cP + dr$$

It is clear that if we can discover values for the coefficients a, b, c and d, this will enable us to predict changes in current account balances from expected changes in national income, prices and interest rates. Thus if we discover that b has a value of 0.1, this means that for every rise of £100 in real income, current account balances will increase by £10, assuming of course that no changes take place in the other variables. A bank may test the effectiveness of the model by using it to forecast future events and by comparing the results with those that actually take place. If the model appears to be a good predictor, it can be used to forecast future movements in current account balances and the bank can judge how it will be affected and plan its future operations accordingly.

USING THESE TOOLS TO GOOD EFFECT

Managers in the future are likely to find increasingly that they need to call on experts to use the tools described in this chapter. Sound judgment and imagination will always be required, but in the competitive race managers will need to know how to use the expertise that management science provides – when to call on this expertise, how to direct it towards banking objectives and how to evaluate the results that are given to them.

Top management next century will be drawn from those entering banking today. All new entrants to banking would be wise therefore to consider what management is about and to seek to learn as much as possible about the ways in which scientific principles can be used to make management efficient and effective.

DISCUSSION QUESTIONS

1. "Management is neither an art nor a science, it is an attitude of mind." Discuss.

2. Consider the differing roles of a Deputy Manager shown in the organisation charts in Fig. 13.

3. In what ways does the sequence of events depicted in Fig. 14 conflict with the procedure established for branch lending in your bank?

4. How could the concept of quality control be applied to the work you are doing? Could the quality be improved and what would be the cost in terms of time and resources?

5. How would you set about measuring the efficiency and effectiveness of three clerks doing similar work? Why might you wish to do this and what would you do with the results you obtained?

6. Consider the ways in which a computer can be used to improve a bank's managerial efficiency.

7. Draw a flow chart for one of the banking operations performed in your office.

8. How might you set about the task of simulating the work of a branch of a large bank? What might be the advantages of doing this?

9. Consider one way in which a mathematical model might be used in your bank.

10. What is a critical path?

Index

Attitude surveys, 66

Bank
- input, 6, 8, 14
- lending, 77
- marketing, 61-70
- objectives, 5
- output, 4, 6
- profits, 5, 6, 9
- services, 2, 4, 65
- system, 1, 2, 15-16, 63

Bar charts, 39
Black Box, 7, 15, 63
Branch management, 26-30
Branch manager, 70
Branch marketing, 68
Break even, 68
Budgetary control, 22, 38
Budget centres, 37

Cairncross, Frances, 70
Charts, 39
Communicating information, 32-47
Communication, 39, 44
Communication strategy, 46
Control, 13, 20
Corporate plan, 17, 24, 33
Corporate planning, 1-11, 24
Cost centres, 37
Costing, 19
Credit cards, 4, 5, 79
Critical Path Analysis (CPA), 79
Cybernetic control, 76

Decision theory, 78
Decision trees, 78
Delegation, 58
Diagrams, 39
Discounted Cash Flow (DCF), 82

Ergonomics, 75
Expected value, 78

Feedback, 9, 38
Flow charts, 77

Gantt chart, 81

Hierarchy of systems, 2
Humble, John, 53
Human development, 53
Human relations, 52
Human resources, 49-58

Index numbers, 43
Information, 32-6, 65
Inputs, 1, 6, 8, 14
Interference, 46
Internal pricing, 37

Job analysis, 56
Job descriptions, 56-7
Job enrichment, 54
Job security, 10
Job specifications, 56

Leadership, 14
Linear programming, 82

Management
- approach, 28
- attitude, 72
- decisions, 8
- definition, 13, 24
- functions, 13, 16-17
- regional, 9
- role, 7
- size, 8, 18
- style, 11

Management by Objectives (MBO), 52, 70
Manpower planning, 8
Marketing mix, 64
Marketing orientation, 61
Market research, 64
Marketing strategy, 61
Mathematical models, 83
McRae, Hamish, 70
Method study, 74
Models, 83
Monitoring, 20, 22

Motivation, 50
Montgomery, Viscount, 25

Network analysis, 79
Net Present Value, 82

Objectives, 1
Office planning, 73
Operational plan, 25
Operational Research (OR), 82
Organisation and Methods (O&M), 73
Organisation chart, 73
Outputs, 1, 4, 6

Packaging, 67
Participation, 21
Pay-back period, 82
Pie diagram, 41
Planning, 13-14, 25-6
  charts, 76
  costs, 20
  flexibility, 11, 20
  spatial, 14, 21
  temporal, 14, 21
Probability, 78
Product
  life cycle, 63-4
  marketing, 66
  pricing, 68
  strategy, 66
  testing, 68
Production orientation, 62
Profit centres, 36
Profit path, 61
Profit planning, 61
Profits, 6, 9
Programme Evaluation and Review Technique (PERT), 79
Public relations, 69

Quality control, 75
Queuing theory, 82

Responsibility centres, 37
Return on Capital Employed (ROCE), 36

Salary administration, 57
Sales campaign, 67
Sales promotion, 67
Sample surveys, 66
Silent salesman, 67
Staff appraisal, 56
Staff selection, 10
Systems, 1, 16, 32

Tactics, 32
Targets, 39, 41, 54
Test marketing, 68
Time study, 75
Top management, 7

Variance analysis, 38

Work measurement, 74
Work study, 73